Motivating Teaching

in higher education with technology

Jay R. Wilson & Edwin G. Ralph
with Shelly Balbar

NEW FORUMS

NEW FORUMS PRESS INC.

Published in the United States of America
by New Forums Press, Inc.1018 S. Lewis St.
Stillwater, OK 74074
www.newforums.com

Copyright © 2014 by New Forums Press, Inc.

All rights reserved. No part of this publication may be reproduced or transmitted in any form or by any means, electronic or mechanical, including photocopy, or any information storage or retrieval system, without permission in writing from the publisher.

Library of Congress Cataloging-in-Publication Data Pending

This book may be ordered in bulk quantities at discount from New Forums Press, Inc., P.O. Box 876, Stillwater, OK 74076 [Federal I.D. No. 73 1123239]. Printed in the United States of America.

ISBN 10: 1-58107-269-4
ISBN 13: 978-1-581072-69-3

Contents

Foreword x
    Purpose 1
    Rationale 2
    Readers 2
    Format 3
    Content 3
Acknowledgements 4

Chapter 1: Essential Motivational Principles 5
    Key Ideas 5
    Learning Motivation 6
        1. Create a Positive Environment 7
        2. Develop Interest 8
        3. Ensure Relevance 8
        4. Build Confidence 9
        5. Employ Meaningful Evaluation 11
    Teaching and Learning 11
    Learning Styles 12
    Motivational Teaching 13
        1. Demonstrate Knowledge 14
        2. Accommodate Learners 15
        3. Manage Prudently 15
        4. Select Appropriate Strategies/Technologies ... 16
        5. Be Flexible 16
        6. Maintain Structure 17
        7. Connect objectives, Tasks, and Evaluation ... 18
        8. Emphasize relevance 18
        9. Create the Learning Climate 19
        10. Maintain Communication 20
        11. Involve Learners 21
        12. Sustain Reflection 21
    Motivating Teaching: A Conceptual Framework ... 22
    Summary 23
    Footnotes 24

Chapter 2: Conditions Conducive to Learning:
Climate and Management 27
    Key Ideas 27
    Creating a Positive Teaching/Learning Climate 28
        1. Portray a Humane Attitude.. 29
        2. Be Honest.. 29
        3. Demonstrate Fairness.. 30
        4. Handle Diversity Equitably....................................... 30
        5. Show Respect.. 31
        6. Build Trust 32
        7. Maintain Curiosity 32
    Ethical and Professional Considerations............................... 33
        Commitment to Students.. 34
        Commitment to Colleagues.. 34
        Commitment to the Institution 34
    The Managerial Process: Organizational Routines
    and Strategies 35
        Management before a Course Begins 35
        Management at the Beginning of a Course................. 38
        Maintaining the Positive Atmosphere......................... 40
        Developing Teaching Instincts 42
    Summary 43
    Footnotes.. 43

Chapter 3: Instructional Practice... 47
    Key Ideas 47
    Planning for Instruction 48
        Rationale for Planning 49
        A Core Principle.. 49
        The Planning Action 50
    Implementing Instruction... 56
        Presenting.. 56
        Questioning... 60
        Key Questioning Competencies.................................... 61
        Responding 64
    Summary 68
    Footnotes.. 68

Chapter 4: Motivating Methods and Technologies 71
Key Ideas 71
Part 1: Teacher-Centered Approaches 72
    Lectures 73
    Implementation 74
    Demonstrations 77
    Discussion 79
    Implementtion: A Distillation of Findings 82
Part 2: Student-Centered Approaches 84
    Small Group Activities 84
    Co-operative Learning 86
    Debates 88
    Drama, Role-Plays, and Simulations 90
    Other Student Centered Strategies 93
Summary 95
Footnotes 95

Chapter 5: Practical Technology Applications
to Enhance Motivation 99
Key Ideas 99
Overview 100
What is Your Motivation? 102
What Technology Will *Not* Do for You 103
Considerations Before Getting Started 104
Moving Forward 106
Impact of Technology on You 108
Technology Tools 110
Critical Questions 111
    Enhance 112
    Obsolesce 112
    Retrieve 112
    Reverse 113
Levels of Technology Integration 113
    Level One: Basic Technologies 113
    Level Two: More Interaction 114
    Level Three: Asynchronous Online Course Delivery 115
What about the Students? 116
Technology and Teaching Using the Internet 117
    Online Discussion Boards 118

Developing a Technology Supported Professional
   Learning Community 120
Ensuring the Success of Your Online Learners.................. 121
   Online Assignments and Assessment......................... 122
You Made It.Now What? 123
Summary 124
Concluding Thoughts: Inspiring Students 125
Footnotes.. 127

References 131

About the Authors 181

Foreword

Purpose

We have created this manual particularly for beginning instructors at the post-secondary level, who have never had formal teacher training. We not only present the essentials of effective instruction that incorporates technology, but in doing so, we review key principles and practices that have been shown to enhance students' motivation to learn. The manual is a distillation of core information derived from both our own professional experience and the body of literature on teaching effectiveness, learning motivation, and the infusion of technology in post-secondary settings. We draw on our respective educational and research backgrounds that range from the elementary through to the college and university levels.

Rationale

Considerable worldwide attention has been given to the importance of improving the teaching/learning process and the incorporation of technology in higher education. Faculty members -- especially those who are newly hired -- are increasingly being expected to promote student learning by exemplifying effective teaching performance as part of their academic duties in colleges and universities. Demands for exemplary teaching that infuses contemporary technologies have arisen among undergraduate student-bodies (and their parents), future employers in business/industry/commerce, university/college administrators, and taxpayers and citizens in general.

Post-secondary institutions have responded by developing a variety of initiatives to meet these challenges, such as: establishing campus-wide instructional development offices; setting up department- or institution-wide teaching centers; conducting seminars/

workshops/courses on specific instructional and technology topics; organizing/presenting regional/national/international teaching/learning conferences; and hiring full- or part-time staff to administer these professional-development events.

In the light of these efforts, we have prepared this handbook to serve as a print resource to support such programs. Moreover, we have also desired to provide -- in a readable and concise format -- a synthesis of several fundamental skills of teaching, an assortment of proven motivational strategies to enhance learning, and a set of sound principles to guide the wise use of instructional technologies, which all instructors in any field could adapt to fit their individual teaching or training contexts.

At the outset we assert our belief that no particular teaching method, no single motivating idea, or no specific technology would be ideally fit all teaching/learning situations. However, we do affirm that the suggestions we offer in this guidebook are grounded both in the current teaching/learning research, and in the actual teaching experiences we have encountered in our educational practice.

Because all instructors are busy, they do not necessarily have the time nor the inclination to review the voluminous literature on teaching, learning, motivation, and educational technology--let alone to attempt to extract pertinent strategies for implementation into their own instructional situations. However, by means of this manual, we believe we have performed a portion of that task for them.

As we did in the 1998 edition of the book (Motivating teaching in higher education, New Forums Press), in this revised version we attempt to write in plain language, avoiding excessive jargon and attempting to clarify educational terms where required. We present what we believe are practical and valuable suggestions for instructors to consider as they plan, prepare, and deliver their respective face-to-face (f2f) and/or online courses and/or class-sessions.

Readers

We have created the manual for all instructional personnel in post-secondary settings interested in enhancing their pedagogical knowledge and skills, but particularly for neophyte practitioners, who may not have not had the opportunity to receive prior professional teacher training. Such individuals may include: newly hired faculty members, sessional lecturers, seminar leaders, laboratory demonstrators, graduate teaching assistants, tutorial leaders, or part-time instructors. Many of the topics would also be of benefit to individuals with duties in apprentice-preparation, coaching, mentoring, supervising, training, managing, or preceptoring in any field of education, business, industry, commerce, health care, sports, or government. These individuals may find the handbook useful in providing empirically-based guidelines for organizing and implementing motivational teaching/learning tasks that incorporate an assortment of technologies.

Format

We present readers with guidelines for infusing various technologies in their preparation and initiation of effective teaching/learning activities. The book helps to answer such questions as: What do I do prior to, at the beginning, during, at the end of, and after the instructional session(s)? The conceptual framework I employed to organize this handbook is based on the two essential functions of the teaching process, the managerial and the instructional aspects. As was the case with the first edition, the present manual is not presented as a research report nor as a regular textbook, but it has an extensive bibliography that refers readers to a host of relevant sources that provide further background.

Content

The content of the handbook chapters is summarized below:

In Chapter 1 we answer the question: "What are the best principles/practices of effective teaching/learning and learner motivation that are applicable to undergraduate education?" We provide key definitions, explain foundational assumptions, and present a conceptual framework for the book.

In Chapter 2 we describe a key component undergirding all motivational instruction: the establishment and maintenance of a positive and productive teaching/learning climate. We also analyze the process of effective classroom management, in terms of the teacher's prior planning and actual implementation of wisely selected instructional procedures and technologies. We also offer strategies and suggestions to deal with interpersonal problems and conflicts that may arise in the teaching/learning process.

In Chapter 3, the heart of the manual, we describe practical components of effective instruction, from both the planning and the implementation aspects. We present specific motivational strategies and possible technologies for conducting both teacher- and learner-centered activities both in f2f and online settings.

In Chapter 4 we distill key insights we derived from our own educational backgrounds and the related literature regarding critical aspects of motivating the teaching/learning process in adult education. We further provide several examples of technologies that have proven effective in these situations.

In Chapter 5 we offer further details to consider when seeking to infuse technologies within the entire teaching/learning process. We conclude the book with insights we have learned regarding the role of technology in post-secondary learning.

Acknowledgements

We wish to thank **Shelly Balbar** for her helpful insights and valuable editorial suggestions in preparing the manuscript. We also thank **Karen Schwier** for her careful editorial proofreading and suggestions regarding early chapter-drafts. Furthermore, we thank **Noah Germaine** for drawing the small clip-cartoons that we inserted throughout the chapters to identify main points and strategic tips. **Edwin** was responsible for drawing the main chapter cartoons, the book's conceptual framework, and the image for the *Adaptive Mentorship* model.

CHAPTER 1

ESSENTIAL MOTIVATIONAL PRINCIPLES

KEY IDEAS

In this chapter, we: (a) discuss the three terms, motivation, learning, and teaching; (b) examine how these processes are related within the instructional setting; and (c) present a conceptual structure, consisting of twelve major principles, which when applied will help guide instructors of f2f and online courses as they plan and implement motivating instructional activities.

In this chapter you will learn:
- Five motivational factors that undergird learning motivation;
- Core definitions of learning and teaching;
- The importance of focusing on learning styles;
- Twelve foundational principles characterizing effective instruction;
- A model conceptualizing the teaching/learning process at the post-secondary;
- Technologies provide motivational tools and techniques to support this process.

Figure 1.0. A key advantage of using information technologies in teaching is their universal access.

Learning Motivation

Teachers in formal educational settings assist students to learn the subject matter in the particular course(s) they teach. However, the challenge of this task is that students may not be motivated to learn, because motivation is a product of a complex blend of individuals' needs, attitudes, competencies, previous experiences, and inherited traits.[1]

Moreover, research suggests that the degree of motivation to learn may be determined by observing the learner's effort to engage in a particular learning activity; and that this effort is influenced by: (a) the value that a learner places on the task, and (b) the expectation the learner has on being successful at it.[2] Because these internal motivational states become deep-rooted in each learner's psyche, teachers ultimately cannot motivate students to do anything. They can only endeavor to affect some of the variables that interact to stimulate students' own motivation to learn.[3]

Learning motivation is affected by a complex blend of learner characteristics.

Researchers in learning motivation further contend that the traditionally held distinction between *extrinsic* (e.g., external reinforcements for student achievement such as grades, awards, privileges, or other tangible rewards) and *intrinsic* motivation (e.g., personal satisfaction, individual enjoyment, feelings of competency, or self-interest) is not as distinguishable as historically proposed.[4] In fact, it is believed that extrinsic reinforcement may be a source of increased self-esteem within an individual, and that this self-esteem in turn serves as a foundation upon which one's intrinsic motivation is further developed.[5] Furthermore, external sources of positive reinforcement (such as: learners' desire for affirmation/confirmation from significant others, desire for recognition, drive for affiliation and belonging, or need for power and competence) may all lead eventually to increased intrinsic motivation in learners.[6]

Thus, rather than trying to diagnose all the complexities of students' psycho/social/emotional make-up, instructors need to be able to apply the motivational principles that have been consistently shown to stimulate student learning. A synthesis of literature on this subject has identified five motivational factors that teachers of all age groups have consistently found effective.[7]

1. Create a Positive Environment[8]

Teachers are responsible for setting the tone of the teaching/learning atmosphere by promoting mutual respect, support, and warmth. When learners believe that they are accepted as worthwhile individuals and as contributing members of the group, and whose affiliation and belonging needs are thereby met, they will then tend to regard the learning tasks of the group with acceptance rather than avoidance. Learning includes not only the cognitive dimension, but also the affective dimension (i.e., the emotions, feelings, and spiritual aspects).

On the other hand, both the research and individuals' own personal experiences have confirmed that teachers who are negatively critical, intimidating, or emotionally cold tend to diminish students' desire to engage in learning activities.[9] In fact, in one survey of 500 graduates from 20 post-secondary institutions who assessed their degree of satisfaction with their undergraduate-education experience, the respondents expressed their greatest dissatisfaction with the institutional climate. They apparently found it non-inviting and unfriendly.[10]

A common fear of beginning instructors, however, is that in their desire to create this pleasant socio-emotional climate, they do not want to appear overly "friendly" for fear their students could somehow see them as weak and/or indecisive, and consequently take advantage of them. However, effective instructors are able to balance this sometimes delicate process. It is possible to maintain a positive, productive teaching/learning environment in f2f and online settings alike, and yet deal with student uncooperative conduct in a direct but respectful manner.[11]

Which of the five essential motivational factors is most important?

2. Develop Interest[12]

Learning motivation is increased when teachers attract and maintain learners' curiosity. Good instructors are skilled both at captivating students' interest early and at stimulating it throughout a term. However, to create and to sustain such motivation requires ingenuity and diligence.

Instructional personnel who are successful at this task do so in many ways. For instance, they may begin a f2f or online class with a puzzling question about the topic; they may project a digital image showing a puzzling scene and ask the group to resolve the apparent discrepancy in the visual; they may introduce a variety of activities/methods/media in one class period in order to immediately engage learner interest; or they may involve learners in active participation from the outset.[13]

3. Ensure Relevance[14]

Motivation to learn is increased when instructors ensure that the content is meaningful to students' lives. Effective instructors are able to provide a convincing argument and a defensible rationale regarding the value of the subject matter or topic being studied. They convey a personal interest in and enthusiasm about their subject, and they provide frequent opportunities for learners to apply their newly acquired knowledge and skills in authentic "real life" situations.

Their instructional decisions demonstrate that: they will adjust the learning activities to meet the developmental needs of the learners; they will model the desired behavior, themselves; they will invite current practitioners from the field (or former students) to be classroom- or online-guests; and they will emphasize that the coursework in which they are engaged is important.[15]

 "Course content must be meaningful to learners."

---

4. Build Confidence

Students' motivation to learn is enhanced when they engage in activities that are optimally balanced between being challenging and being achievable. A goal of the teaching process is that the teacher will eventually make him/herself unneeded, in that the learners will ultimately internalize the material or master the skills so that the instructor will no longer be required to assist in the learner's development.[16]

TIP
The objectives, activities, and evaluation must be congruent.

During this process, teachers apply both their technical (knowledge or task) and supportive (human relations) skills in inverse proportions, respectively, to match the learners' developmental level in performing a specific task or in applying certain knowledge. The learner's developmental level consists of two dimensions: his/her competence and his/her confidence in acquiring a body of knowledge, or performing a particular learning task or skill set.[17] That is, if learners' competence to perform the task or to solve a problem is low, then the teacher reciprocates by meeting the students' needs for direction by giving clear, specific guidance, high task orientation, and concise, orderly directions -- in short, by using "telling" behaviors. Correspondingly, if a learner's confidence, assurance, or self-efficacy in performing the task is low, then the instructor acts by meeting the learner's need for bolstered confidence by providing highly supportive and encouraging responses.

On the other hand, when the learners' development level of mastering a particular body of knowledge or a skill set increases (i.e., when their task-specific competence and confidence levels rise, then the instructor, coach, or mentor reciprocates by reducing his/her application of the two leadership style components, (i.e., the

The New Forums Better Teaching Series / 9

technical/task dimension, and the supportive/encouraging aspect) in order to match the learners' existing level of ability.

Throughout this developmental learning process, the effective teacher/mentor provides an appropriate blend of directive and supportive responses to synchronize, in inverse proportions, with the particular competence and confidence levels of the learner to perform a particular skill set. As the learner's developmental level advances, the mentor decreases the degree of task-direction, reinforcement, feedback and guidance given to the student in performing that task. In turn, the learner/protégé – acknowledging her/his newly acquired levels of task-specific competence and confidence – is then able to set new learning goals for other tasks at higher levels of achievement. The cycle is then repeated with other learning goals.

To illustrate how this mentorship process operates, we have produced a model called Adaptive Mentorship,[18] which we formerly called Contextual Supervision. In our workshops, within which we disseminate the model, we make use of power-point technology to insert moving arrows to illustrate how a mentor would adapt his/her mentoring response to match, in a reciprocal fashion, the protégé's skill-specific developmental stage.

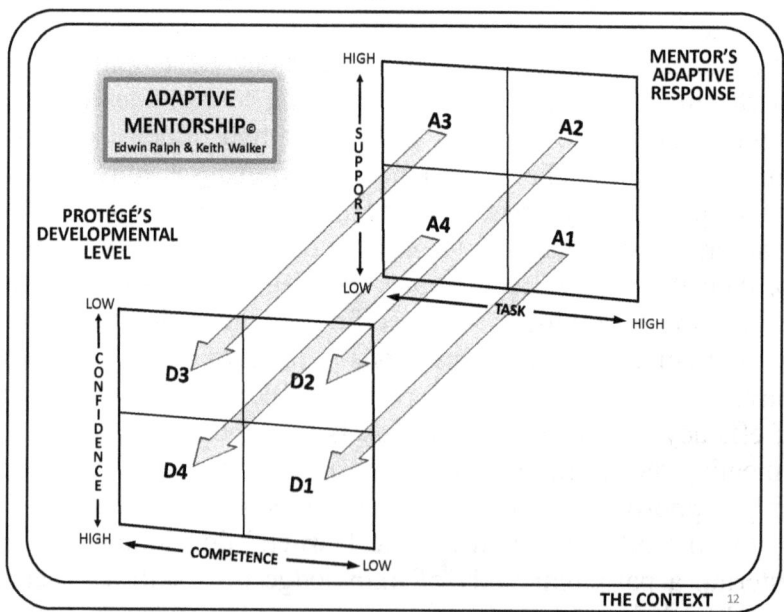

Figure 1.1. Adaptive Mentorship©. The mentor matches his/her adaptive response to synchronize with the skill-specific developmental level of his/her protégé. (Ralph & Walker, 2010, 2012, 2013).

5. Employ Meaningful Evaluation

Students' motivation to learn is increased when they experience a sense of achievement for accomplishing the learning goals.[19] If the instructor designs the teaching/learning activities by incorporating the four motivational principles described above, then learners will tend to engage in the tasks in order to complete them successfully. If the evaluation activities in a course are consistent both with the initial instructional objectives and the type of daily learning activities experienced by the learners, and if the evaluation feedback received is perceived to be fair and authentic, then learners typically will have a desire to pursue the goals.[20] The reward for this learning achievement may be intrinsic (e.g., the inner glow of satisfaction for succeeding at a task), or extrinsic (e.g., high grades, awards, peer- or teacher-approval, or confirmation from others).[21]

Key principles for instructors to apply as they reinforce learners' achievement is that the reinforcement, to be effective, must be: (a) genuine (i.e., provided for clearly describable progress, not given indiscriminately or to be perceived by learners as artificial or un-earned); (b) immediate (i.e., provided at the time of the successful task completion); and specific (i.e., reinforcing particular points in the task performance rather than administering vague or general praise); (c) constructive (i.e., students receive input related to what they are or are not doing in relation to the task) .[22]

Teaching and Learning

In this manual, we conceptualize learning as a relatively permanent change in learners' behavior as a result of repeated experience.[23] Learning can occur without teaching, and vice versa. However, in formal educational settings, the act of teaching is assumed to promote students' learning.[24]

All technologies must promote learning.

Traditionally, post-secondary teaching was seen as telling, lecturing, and expert presenting via one-way, instructor-directed communication. Accordingly, learning was perceived to be the passive reception of such teaching, whereby learners sat dutifully listening, copying verbatim notes from the lecture, and subsequently memorizing and regurgitating the material on formal examinations, after which learners quickly forgot the information.

However, in recent years there has emerged a growing trend to reform the transmission process to one exhibiting the following characteristics: [25]

- the communication act becoming more interactive and collaborative among all students and teachers;
- the teacher becoming more of a facilitator of student learning, and less of a dispenser of knowledge;
- the incorporation of active-learning methods (e.g., cooperative group learning activities, technological tools, and inquiry-based tasks) becoming more common.

Educators are searching for creative ways to organize learning and make learning more meaningful. Many educators question the value of using the lecture method in any form to promote the learning process while others even believe that the term teacher, itself, is archaic and repressive, and should be replaced by other terms such as facilitator or guide.[26]

The term teaching, as we use it in this manual, represents the entire decision-making process by which an instructor plans, prepares, organizes, implements, and assesses a variety of methods, technologies, activities, and events for the purpose of promoting student learning.[27] When these decisions are enacted with clarity, precision, and consideration, we believe that teachers can enhance students' motivation to learn.[28] In the entire process, instructors must ensure that the fundamental integrity of the learner is not violated.[29]

Learning Styles

By virtue of our human nature and our unique personalities, each person has a particular learning preference.[30] These preferences or styles have been studied and categorized by several researchers into a variety of learning style structures. For instance, one approach[31] classifies people, according to their dominant learning style, into four categories: (a) if they prefer concrete experience they could be called Active Pragmatists; (b) if they prefer reflective observation they could be called Cautious Reflectors; (c) if they prefer abstract conceptualization they could be called Analytical Theorists; or (d) if they prefer active experimentation they could be called Active Learners. Others researchers classify learners as falling into varying degrees on a range of scales such as Independent/Dependent, Competitive/Collaborative, or Avoidant/Participant.[32]

The advantages for instructors of being aware of learning styles are that: (a) they can better understand the differences among learners; (b) they should adjust their teaching to accommodate these differences; and (c) they can be explicit with this information for learners so that all participants will realize that learning style offers a legitimate explanation for classroom diversity.[32]

Potential dangers of over-emphasizing the learning style research in one's teaching, however, are that: (a) most people do not fall entirely within one category; (b) instructors realistically do not have the time nor resources to diagnose each learner's preference, let alone design individualized learning activities for each student to match his/her unique learning profile; or (c) instructors catering only to learners' preferred style will do little to enhance development in lesser developed areas of the students' cognitive abilities, and may rather serve to label or categorize them permanently.[33] A key implication of the knowledge of learning styles for instructional planning is that effective teachers will select a variety of materials, methods, and technologies as a means of providing all learners with an opportunity to work within their learning context.[34]

Motivational Teaching

We have created a set of twelve factors that characterize effective instruction. These principles interact with and complement each other, and work together synergistically. Often, effective teachers demonstrate them consciously, but at other times they appear to perform these tasks subconsciously.

The following dozen characteristics form a necessary foundation upon which exemplary teaching is built. However, these basic attributes alone are not sufficient to produce effective teaching/learning: the whole is more than the sum of its parts. We specifically show where implementing technology can be a contributing factor in promoting teaching and learning.[35]

1. Demonstrate Knowledge[36]

Effective instructors understand and apply knowledge from three essential sources: the content from their subject-matter specialty; the field of general pedagogy (basic teaching methods); and the unique area that encompasses specialized, content-specific instructional strategies.

What is a disadvantage of emphasizing the importance of learning styles?

Historically, it was believed that if instructors in post-secondary institutions knew their content, then they would naturally be good at teaching it. People's personal experience has repeatedly shown that this assumption is simply not the case. We have all encountered teachers who were highly knowledgeable in their subject field, but who could not present it in a clear or interesting manner. Yet, the reverse situation could also be true: a teacher could be technologically skilled and motivationally prepared, but if his/her knowledge of the subject matter knowledge was inadequate, then his/her credibility as an effective instructor would be questioned.

Furthermore, effective teachers also know how to apply a set of generic pedagogical methods common to all subjects. In addition, they possess and apply a third element of knowledge consisting of a combination of Pedagogical Content Knowledge (PCK)[37] and Technical Pedagogical Content Knowledge (TPACK).[38] Effective teachers have developed a specific expertise that is unique to the particular discipline, program, and/or course they teach. Over time, as they have reflected upon and interacted with this subject matter, they have devised certain instructional tactics and techniques that apply directly to specific concepts or difficult points in the course. For instance, they come to know precisely where students will typically encounter difficulties, and they will have generated effective technological supports to assist learners to understand and resolve these potential problems. An example of this technological support would be.

When teachers skillfully apply these three knowledge bases, they positively influence their students' motivation to engage in learning. Thus, to demonstrate good teaching entails much more than merely accumulating knowledge.

2. Accommodate Learners[39]

Effective teachers realize that no single teaching method or technology is sufficient to help all students learn. Employing a variety of approaches and media is necessary to adapt the content to meet the diversity of learning styles.[40] Skillful teachers are able to adjust their teaching style to match students' development levels: they teach to promote student understanding and development.

Thus, when instructors make provision in their procedures to move learners from the known to the unknown, from the concrete to the abstract, and from the simple to the complex, then students experience both the challenge and the success that facilitate learning. Skilled teachers reflectively adapt their instructional strategy to accommodate learner diversity. As a consequence, students' motivation to learn is promoted. An example[41] of incorporating technology to accommodate students' diverse learning preferences would be creating videos or podcasts of lectures. These resources would allow students who work better outside of the traditional learning environment to be more successful.

3. Manage Prudently[42]

Effective instructors convey that they have planned and organized + routines and procedures in such a way as to create the conditions conducive for teaching and learning. They tend to exude an air of composure and they demonstrate competence. They typically handle disruptions with a calm demeanor. They are approachable and friendly, yet they maintain a business-like deportment in their interrelationships. They tend to have authority without appearing as controlling or coercive; and they consistently model the values and behaviors that they wish their students to express.[42]

Furthermore, on the basis of studies of responses from a variety of students at various educational levels,[43] students seem to desire the following attributes in their teachers and professors to:
- teach well
- keep order
- explain clearly
- be interesting
- treat students fairly
- be friendly.

It is interesting to note that half of these response categories were related to the teachers' class management and human relations skills.

4. Select Appropriate Strategies/ Technologies[44]

Instructors who are recognized as successful consistently incorporate a variety of strategies that help motivate students. They incorporate technology for the purposes of stimulating student thinking, making clear presentations, providing meaningful interaction, and connecting learning objectives, activities, and evaluation.[45]

Instructors integrate these events and technologies to maintain participants' motivation in the learning process. With such an increasing array of new and developing technologies, instructors should realize that they cannot use them all integrate them all, but that they it would be wiser to plan carefully to employ fewer technologies that have proven to be of interest to students.

5. Be Flexible[46]

A typical novice instructor may carefully plan and conduct a f2f or online class session, but may become fixated on having to complete the agenda as prepared, despite changing conditions. Thus, the instructor may miss or ignore the opportunity to take advantage of a spontaneous teachable moment or an unforeseen chance to enhance student understanding. The instructor may feel compelled to follow his/her plan rigidly. On the other hand, effective instructors are able to provide for flexibility in their teaching, allowing for an occasional tangent without derailing the overall direction for a class session. They have developed their inner sense to know when such a diversion will be worthwhile for the group.

This allowance for flexibility developed through the wisdom of experience helps instructors accommodate unique learning backgrounds.[47] They are not uncomfortable with uncertainties, and they are able to capitalize

TIP
Instructors must simultaneously display structure and flexibility.

on diversions and mistakes in a positively constructive manner. They convey that errors are steps to improvement, and they are willing to take such risks, signaling to learners that confidence and competence do not emerge fully perfected.

Flexibility is also present in the new type of course that is offered partially or wholly online. An appealing point for such courses is their responsiveness to the needs of students. This responsiveness in turn means a new approach to teaching, whereby the instructor must also be prepared to address a variety of issues.[48]

6. Maintain Structure[49]

Although successful instructors may not be fixated on following a set prescription for learning, they do have an overall blueprint for the session. They move the agenda along at a comfortable pace, confirming what research has consistently indicated: to maintain a brisk momentum in the activities influences student motivation more positively than does slowing the pace down.[50] A slower pace typically causes tedium, boredom, and potential management problems, whereas a quicker progression helps keep the majority of students alert.

Other characteristics of competent instructor planning patterns are that: learning objectives are made explicit; appropriate technologies are utilized; transitions and summaries are clearly stated; assignments are clearly explained; and task procedures and expectations are systematically described.[51]

Whether instructors select teacher-centered or learner-centered approaches, and whether they are f2f or web-based in nature, they ensure that key points and procedures are clear to all participants.

Effective instructors apply this type of planning over a range of time frames: daily, weekly, monthly, or term schedules.[52] By having an overall structure experienced and novice instructors alike articulate explicitly what students will learn or be able to do as a result of the particular learning experience(s).

Planning fills an even more important role for individuals teaching with an emphasis on technology or in a non-traditional delivery mode.[53] Due to the need to create digital resources with little or no previous guidance, or to reformat existing resources, instructors will find that planning and development often take much longer. Issues such as dealing with online copyright and allowing extra time for students to receive permissions present other planning challenges.

> 🍎 *No single technology is sufficient to facilitate all learning.*

7. Connect Objectives, Tasks, and Evaluations[54]

Skilled instructors not only are able to conceptualize clear learning objectives for students, but they explicitly identify them at the beginning of a course or class. They connect how the tasks of the session will help accomplish these objectives, and they also make use of web-based materials and online learning management systems to provide advanced organizers and evaluation material. Furthermore, in the case of evaluating student achievement, teachers ensure that assessment activities reflect both the instructional objectives and the previous learning tasks. Effective post-secondary instructors indicate to students early what assignments are required, how they will be graded, and what performance standards are expected.[55]

The reasons for ensuring that learning objectives, activities, and assessments are congruent are that all participants will understand the expectations of the activities; all will know how learner performance will be evaluated; students will know exactly what they will learn and be expected to do; and instructors will be perceived as being organized and fair, so that students will not feel disadvantaged.[56] As a result, the instructor's credibility will be enhanced, and learners will take increasing responsibility to become more self-evaluative about their coursework. Motivation to learn will thus be stimulated.

8. Emphasize Relevance[57]

Effective instructors consistently relate the subject matter to the students' personal experiences. For instance, they will take time to explain how the content may help students in the future; how the course fits in with other disciplines; or how it may connect to learners' personal lives and experiences. Because technology is pervasive in the lives of students, effective instructors attempt to keep up with advancements in the field. Social networking, blogging, and video sharing can draw students closer to the content at hand, and bolster motivation. When students perceive that a certain topic is meaningful and that instructors connect it to their real world, their interest is piqued.

Digital course content and an expanding number of web-based sources of content specific material allow instructors to tailor the material to suit learners' needs and styles. Today's generation is largely familiar with technology, and when instructors implement it (e.g., with podcasts, videos, and social networking sites), they are able to make course content more appealing.

9. Create the Learning Climate[58]

The ability of instructors to build and maintain positive interpersonal relationships is one of the key elements in determining teaching/learning effectiveness. When participants in an online or f2f class sense that they are welcomed, accepted, and respected by their instructor and peers, their motivation to learn is enhanced. Instructors cannot help but convey their attitude and presence, either visibly in f2f classes or virtually in online environments, by how they treat and care for students.

Certain attributes and characteristics have been repeatedly identified[59] among populations of effective teachers for creating positive online and face-to-face learning environments, such as: enthusiasm, empathy, warmth, fairness, openness, and task-orientation.

However, when such lists of traits are identified, two possible risks arise. One danger, particularly for beginning teachers, is that they may interpret the list as being prescriptive rather than descriptive. They may misconstrue the idea that in order to become an effective instructor they must make major changes in their personality to conform to some "idealized image of the paragon of professional perfection." They may consequently fail to realize that a key ingredient to becoming a proficient instructor is to "be yourself,"

Should traits of effective teaching be interpreted descriptively or prescriptively?

to be genuine, and to build on the strengths one already possesses.[60] Another potential danger is to conclude from the lists of positive traits that good instructors do not experience human relations problems in their courses. In fact, all instructional personnel experience their share of class management or interpersonal difficulties and seek satisfactory ways to remedy them.

Online learning environments (either full or blended courses) have their own management issues. Managing the learning climate in these online types may generate difficulties, because the traditional ways of interacting are not present. Non-verbal communication is replaced by emoticons or smileys. The idea of transactional distance also becomes more significant in that the farther away the student feels from the action, the less connected they are to the class.[61] Instructors need to pay particular attention to ensuring they create a welcoming climate in these learning contexts. A difference between effective and ineffective instructors is that the former do not ignore these issues, but that they deal with them deliberately and directly, and that they concentrate on preventive strategies more than they do on remedial or curative ones.

10. Maintain Communication[62]

Effective teachers are explicit in communicating their course procedures and expectations. When instructors post instructions online or in hard copy, with respect to course activities, assignments, or other learning tasks, they do so in a precise manner. Nothing is left to misinterpretation, and vague and ambiguous terms are avoided. Instructors encourage students to make contact through email, videoconferencing, social media, and other digital communication tools.

In f2f settings effective instructors use their voice well: volume, tone, projection, pitch, articulation, and pronunciation are appropriate and clear. When giving explanations, they provide examples related to students' experiences, and they break the particular content into appropriately sized segments, so that learners can readily assimilate the material. When providing feedback to learners, effective instructors ensure that students know exactly how well they have performed, and they also ensure that learners understand the evaluation standards and criteria.

Technology allows for excellent opportunities to communicate with learners. E-mail, online discussions, blogs, and mobile devices can all be used to help the instructor and students to be more accessible to one another. These technological means of instant communication give opportunities to students to immediately share ideas and seek input from instructors.[63]

11. Involve Learners[64]

From the outset of the first class session effective instructors ensure that learners are actively engaged in meaningful learning experiences. This is not to infer that all learning activities will be student-centered; in fact, they are proficient at employing a variety of methods and technologies. An example of using technology to actively engage learners would be.to use an online polling system on student's smartphones to generate their input on a lecture topic or an event that effects their daily lives.

12. Sustain Reflection[65]

A key trait undergirding effective instructors' practice is their ability to analyze and reflect on their own teaching performance. This reflection enables them to consider better ways to motivate students' learning within a specific environmental context, and instructors perform this self-analysis and self-reflection on a continual basis, often in the midst of the daily routines of instructional life.

On the basis of these internal processes they make instructional decisions sometimes instantaneously, sometimes at the end of a session in preparation for an upcoming class, or sometimes in revising plans for the following year. They reflect to improve their own professional practice, and they make adjustments in their own instructional or management behaviors, advise students to adjust their own thinking or behavior, or modify materials, media, or technology on the basis of this reflection. Specific examples of instructors using technology to enhance this reflective process are: (a) digitally recording their reactions regarding a just-completed class; (b) reviewing a video recording made by a peer-mentor of their recent class session; or (c) sharing recent teaching experiences and insights with a peer via their laptop webcam programs.

Motivating Teaching: A Conceptual Framework

In the preceding sections we have summarized the principles that sustain effective teaching practice with an emphasis on the impact of motivation and awareness of technology on learning. The following visual serves as a graphic conceptual framework that incorporates the above-mentioned principles as the foundation upon which effective instruction is designed.

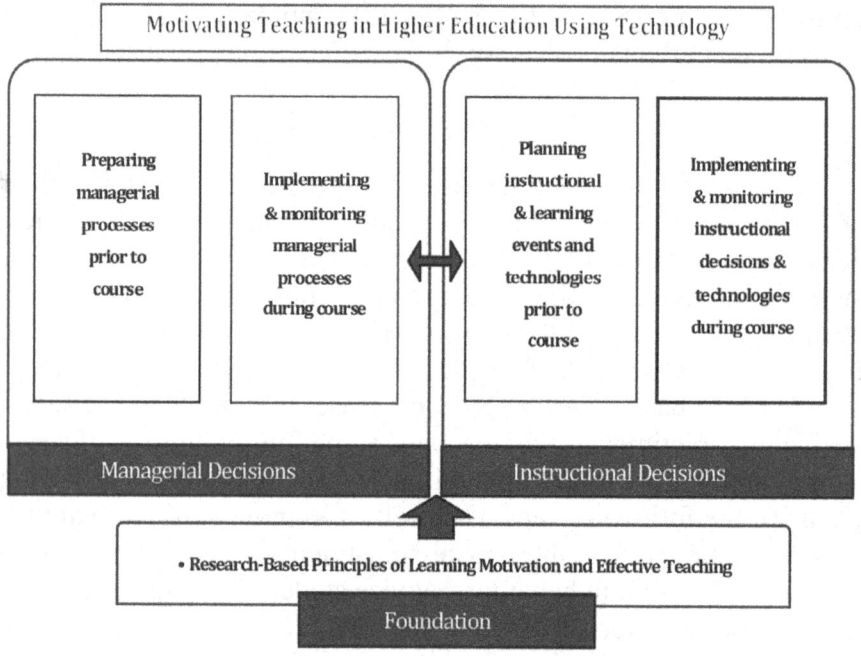

Figure 1.2. Motivational Teaching: Conceptual Framework

Figure 1.2 depicts how we conceptualize effective teaching/learning at the post-secondary level. We also use the visual to organize the structure of this handbook. The teaching/learning process takes place without the instructors or the students being overly concerned about categorizing the activities into managerial or instructional components: they simply engage in the entire process during the daily routines of classroom life.

Figure 1.2 shows that for investigative purposes effective teaching may be classified into two basic categories: (a) the managerial side (i.e., what the instructor says and does to create and maintain the necessary conditions under which effective teaching and learning can proceed); and (b) the instructional aspect (i.e., what the teacher does and says to plan, prepare, present and assess motivational teaching/learning activities and technologies).

> *"Motivational teaching has instructional and managerial dimensions."*

One can also see from Figure 1.0 that a key factor undergirding these two sub-components is the teaching/learning climate. We describe this climate as the psycho/social/emotional tone for which the teacher has the ultimate responsibility of establishing and maintaining in the class, lab, online discussion board, wiki, or wherever the learning activities take place. In essence, Figure 1.0 represents the idea that developing effective teaching is contingent upon the instructor's consistent integration of effective teaching, motivation, and technology.

SUMMARY

By now you should have a broader understanding of motivation and how it impacts your teaching and your students' learning. It is important to actuate what you are learning in this manual and put it into practice. Take the time to reflect on each of the elements we have presented in this chapter to see how you structure your courses. Have you created a climate of success in your learning environments? What can you feel comfortable about and where do you need to direct your efforts. How do the twelve factors we share in this chapter fit with your personal philosophy of teaching. Perhaps you have already made an effort to incorporate them into your approach to teaching. Compare the model we have presented to your specific teaching situation to see how the many elements in your courses coexist. Addressing these issues will provide you with a strong foundation for increasing and enhancing motivation in your teaching.

In the next chapter we will introduce you to ways to create a positive learning environment and how to manage the day-to-day operations of your classroom.

Footnotes

[1] Ames & Ames (1984); Ryan (2013); Stipek (2002); Weimer (1996d)

[2] Anderson et al. (2009); Draves (2007); Gorges & Kandler (2012)

[3] Chen & Kao (2012); de Charms (1984); Styer (2009)

[4] Frith (n.d.); Rueda (2011); Ryan & Deci (2002)

[5] Anderson et al. (2009); Dembo (2013); Pappas (2013a, 2013b)

[6] Dwaraka (2013); Joyce et al. (2009); Rubie-Davies (2011)

[7] Frith (n.d.); Gardner (1993); Martin (2014)

[8] Bennett & Scholes (2001); Eble (1994); Garavan et al. (2010)

[9] Driscoll (2009); Education in America (2013); Gom (2009)

[10] The landscape (1994)

[11] Ginsberg & Wlodkowski (2009); Jarrett Thoms (n.d.)

[12] Hidi et al. (1992); McLaughlin (2010); Reio & Wiswell (2000)

[13] Graham & Weiner (2012); Malamed (2011); Robinson & Schraw (2008)

[14] Bell et al. (2013); Fullan (2012, 2013); Hsu & Hamilton (2010); Kember & McNaught (2007); Pace (2012)

[15] Jarvis (2006); Kates (2012)

[16] Blanchard et al. (2010); Jackson (2011); Kahan Kennedy, & Hinkley (2011); Lockyer et al. (2010); Ralph & Walker (2012)

[17] Daloz (2012); Hubball et al. (2010); Johansson et al. (2012); Ralph & Walker (2013)

[18] Feldman et al. (2010); Johansson et al. (2011); Kalén et al. (2010); Ralph & Walker (2011); Ruru et al. (2013)

[19] Angelo (1991, 1993); But I made (1996); Joyce et al. (2009); Miller (2012)

[20] Berliner & Calfee (2004); Cronin (1993)

[21] Ames & Ames (1984); Biggs & Tang (2011)

[22] Dweck (2002); McMillan (2002); Ng, L. et al. (2011); Rohrbacher (2012)

[23] Frazee & Rudnitski (1995); Joyce et al. (2009); Meyer et al. (2010); Mezirow (1991); Ralph (1998)

24 Knowles et al. (2005); Skrabut (2013); Stronge (2007)

25 Case et al. (1994); Kennedy et al. (2010); Minocha & Roberts (2011); Stewart (1993, 1994); Weimer (1996a)

26 Barr & Tagg (2004); Gardner (1983, 2000); Jeffries & Skidmore (2010); Tapscott (2002)

27 Burden & Byrd (2012); Glancy & Isenberg (2011); Windschitl (2002)

28 Good (1990); Slavin (2011); Sternberg (1987, 1994, 1997)

29 Barr & Tagg (2004); Howles (2007); Hsu & Hamilton (2010); Niedzlek-Feaver & Black (2012); Truebridge (2014)

30 Ahedo (2011); Collins (2011); Cornett (1983)

31 Ralph (1998); Sims & Sims (1996a, 1996b)

32 Graf & Liu (2009); Sims & Sims (1995a, 1995b); Solvie & Sungur (2012)

33 Grasha (1996); Grasha & Yangarber-Hicks (2000); Grasha-Riechmann (n.d.); Huang et al. (2008); McMillan et al. (2002)

34 Kyei-Blankson et al. (2009); Parkay et al. (2014); Sternberg & Williams (2010)

35 Arvidson (2008); Greer & Mott (2011); Mishra & Koehler (2006); Wohlfarth et al. (2012)

36 Burden & Byrd (2012); Stronge (2007)

37 Cavin (2008); Hattie & Yates (2013); Mayer (2001)

38 Benson & Ward (2013); Harris & Hofer (2011); Pappas (2013d); Shin et al. (2009)

39 Al-Ajlan (2012); Elliott et al. (2000); Merriam et al. (2007); Roesky & Kennepohl (2008)

40 Chen et al. (2008); Commons et al. (1984); Yang & Richardson (2010)

41 Roberts (2010)

42 Bergin (2001); Jarvis (2006); Schon (1995)

43 Heller (2013); Medina (2008); Snowman et al. (2012)

44 Burns-Sardone (2008); Cruickshank & Haefele (2002); Osborne & Kriese (2012); Proulx (2012)

45 Angelo (1991); Smith (2007)

46 Banas (2011); Gross Davis (2009); Rolf (2012)

47 Anton-Oldenburg (2002); Kurucz (2006); OER (n.d.)

48 Amabile & Kramer (2011); Ralph & Walker (2011); Sergiovanni (1992); University of British Columbia (2011)

49 Beidler (1986, 2011)

[50] Ralph (1998, 2004); University of Saskatchewan (2008); Weimer (1996d)

[51] Burden & Byrd (2012); Eggen & Kauchak (2012); Ralph (2004); Slavin (2011)

[52] Heick (2013); Ogrenci (2012); Ralph (2004)

[53] Abdallah (2011); Berry (2011); Harasim (2012); Lewis (2000); Micarelli et al. (2011); Stevens & Kitchenham (2011)

[54] Belloni & Christian (2012); Morgan (2012); Worthen (1993)

[55] American Association (1996); Guskey (1996); McMillan (2002); Vogt & Schaffner (2012)

[56] Cho et al. (2011); Curzon (2004)

[57] Menchaca & Bekele (2008); Smyth & Volker (2013); Truebridge (2014)

[58] Andrews et al. (2011)

[59] Chou (2010); Mentkowski et al. (2000); Stronge (2007)

[60] Jarrett Thoms (n.d.); Ralph & Konchak (1996)

[61] Albon & Trinidad (2002); Calbraith & Dennick (2011); Frederick (1987); Murphy (1999); Murphy & Ángeles Rodríguez-Manzanares (2008); Nihalani & Shah (2012)

[62] Arikan (2012)

[63] Allen & Seaman (2010); Angelov et al. (2010)

[64] Abdallah (2011); Brooks (1987); Garavan et al. (2010); Stice (1987)

[65] Burden & Byrd (2012); Daloz et al. (1996); Danielson (2007); Hope (2011); Stronge (2007)

CHAPTER 2

CONDITIONS CONDUCIVE TO LEARNING: CLIMATE AND MANAGEMENT

KEY IDEAS

In Chapter 2, we present specific strategies for instructors to incorporate in order to create a positive teaching/learning climate, and to establish and maintain an appropriate learning-management plan.

In this chapter you will learn:
- Six strategies that help create and maintain a positive/productive learning climate;
- Three ethical considerations undergirding effective teaching/learning;
- Specific strategies and approaches for both establishing and sustaining a stable organizational environment;
- Early and ongoing strategies that engage learners and promote collegial and productive learning.

Figure 2.0. Which of the memos on the screens is correct?

Creating a Positive Teaching/Learning Climate

A key factor that links the managerial and instructional functions of effective teaching is the presence of a positive socio-emotional environment pervading the teaching-learning setting. The onus rests upon instructors to establish and maintain such a working relationship.[1] By virtue of their legal, professional, and ethical position, instructors have been hired to teach/facilitate a course or program.

**TIP
Instructors are responsible to create a positive learning climate.**

How does one create this positive and productive climate? To answer this critical question we present six strategies shown to promote an appealing learning atmosphere.

1. Portray a Humane Attitude

The teaching-learning process involves both intelligence and emotions. When instructors demonstrate sensitivity to the non-academic interests and needs of students, they begin to create an accepting climate conducive to learning.[2] Furthermore, they tend to demonstrate their genuine interest in students by what they say and do, both in f2f and online settings. They exhibit a professional yet approachable manner in their relationships by consistently showing empathy and understanding, especially when students raise questions or concerns and they deal with them privately or publicly, as required.

Humane instructors not only understand that technology is an integral aspect of students' lives today, but they further demonstrate this sensitivity by permitting students to connect freely via various mobile devices and portable computers. Further ways that instructors can demonstrate their caring attitude are: (a) respecting students and their views; (b) incorporating students' ideas into learning situations; (c) being available by ensuring that they arrive for class early or leave later so that they may dialogue with students; (d) keeping office hours; and (e) admitting errors.[3]

2. Be Honest[4]

When teachers gain a reputation for being truthful, students become less cynical about how they may be treated, and also less suspicious about possible hidden agendas. Presenting the subject matter accurately, examining alternative viewpoints, avoiding dogmatism, withholding judgment, and maintaining honesty in conducting research and reporting results are all examples of professors' behaviour that promote the development of trust within the student/teacher relationship.

Research[5] among adult students has revealed five indicators of "instructor authenticity" (i.e., the perception among students that their teachers are honest and open with them): (a) Maintaining congruence between words and actions; (b) revealing aspects of their personality; (c) accepting students' suggestions and being willing to incorporate them into the program; (d) disclosing the full agenda of a course and all of its expectations early; and (e) being willing to acknowledge their own mistakes.

3. Demonstrate Fairness[6]

Key factors influencing fairness with students are consistency and impartiality. For instance, to prevent major inconsistencies from arising, instructors teaching several sections of one course should collaborate in setting common course goals and assessment standards. In both f2f and online courses, instructors need to be seen as showing no favouritism by providing individual attention equally; requesting monopolizers to permit others to contribute; avoiding stereotyping or discriminating for any reason--and stopping students who do so.

4. Handle Diversity Equitably[7]

Effective teachers take consistent and deliberate action to apply fairness in daily practice. By doing so, they model how to interact with diverse students and work at removing barriers of exclusion and alienation. Sensitive instructors are, first, aware of unacceptable practices that mitigate against the acceptance of diversity, and second they counteract these negative patterns with specific and overt responses. Some educators suggest that these types of diversity issues may not be as evident in online environments as they are when people are physically together.

Gender issues.[8] Effective teachers are aware that gender biases exist, and to help eliminate them they may discuss these issues with their classes. Furthermore, during the teaching/learning situation, instructors will ensure, on a consistent basis, that they: call on female students as often as males, listen attentively to all students' contributions, ask a variety of questions of all students, allow adequate wait-time for all participants to answer, and convey a spirit of concern and understanding for all students. Using such language is not just a matter of being politically correct, but of advocating *and* practicing fairness and equality.

Multicultural issues.[9] Effective instructors imbue minority students with a sense of belonging, while respecting their ethnic or cultural differences. They recognize similarities and differences between and among diverse groups, and they stress the former. Online or in the classroom, they will not tolerate overt racism, ethnic slurs, or disparaging comments against anyone. Teachers who do so are serious about reducing stereotyping and about celebrating what all individuals share – not just what makes them distinct.

Students with disabilities.[10] If the fundamental norms of fairness, respect, and human understanding are prevalent in a learning situation in which any students with disabilities participate, then there is little opportunity for inappropriate or discriminatory reactions to develop against them. However, unintentional misinterpretations, stereotypes or negative feelings may occasionally arise, but effective instructors are sensitive to students with disabilities.

People with disabilities do not want to be treated differently, and yet from both the legal, moral and sometimes practical standpoint, instructors are obliged to accommodate the special needs of these individuals. Based on a desire to help equalize the opportunities in assisting these individuals, responsible instructors will incorporate modifications in the delivery and/or format of the course. For example, alternative arrangements may be made for student examinations (such as posting all course material to the internet, allowing digital coding of lectures/readings for later review online or podcasting, or electronic note taking). Moreover, during regular class, lessons provision may be made for the use of an interpreter, tutor, reader, or auxiliary material and equipment. Students with disabilities do not want to receive prejudicial treatment, but they do want to participate in learning on an equal playing field, which may require accommodation.

5. Show Respect[11]

Students repeatedly report[12] that when they sense that instructors acknowledge them as worthwhile individuals with unique ideas and talents to contribute to the learning situation, their interest and motivation regarding the subject increases. Students want their instructors to treat them with respect, and to respond to their inquiries and questions seriously. They, as do their instructors, wish to be granted consideration, civility, and courtesy in their working relationships. Such instructors deal with teacher-student conflicts in private: they do not let problems with one or two of their students interfere with or detract from the positive relationships that have been developed with the great majority of the group who are productively engaged in the learning activities.

6. Build Trust[13]

Skilled teachers foster a climate of trust among class members; however, trust is especially important in virtual learning settings where there is less opportunity to informally create and/or build relationships. The building of trust and respect in a group is not the product of implementing any single technique, but results from an accumulation of events over time. Trust must be earned. In this process, instructors begin to share some of their authority, while simultaneously maintaining their credibility (i.e., still being perceived as knowledgeable, competent, expert, but also as helpful and patient). This process also entails being open about critiquing ones' own weaknesses.

Instructors build authenticity by accepting learners' inputz.

Students readily perceive whether or not an instructor is nurturing the trust relationship by granting them voice, by being a genuine listener, by showing interest in their lives, and by balancing support with challenge. Exemplary instructors maintain a deliberate professional distance in their relationship with students: they may attend students' social or athletic events, but they refrain from becoming overly familiar, or from joining students' online social networks. They do not appear solely as buddies, or as "one among equals."

 "Trust must be earned."

7. Maintain Consistency[14]

An essential component of producing an agreeable working climate in a learning group is for leaders to demonstrate their integrity and credibility by keeping their word. With distance-delivered courses, the web site may be the only contact the student has with the instructor. Effective instructors maintain consistency between what they declare and what they do in such elements as the course syllabus, the evaluation procedures, the comment schedule, or commitments made to students.

Keeping one's promises not only enhances one's credibility but it bolsters the trust relationship. Research[15] among adult learners has shown that students will tolerate a wide variety of teaching styles and approaches, provided that a climate of trust has been formed in the relationship. Students will place confidence in instructors' experience and competence if the latters' words are congruent with their behaviours.

The six behavioural norms just presented have been identified, both in the research and in practical classroom experience, as promoting the growth of a harmonious working atmosphere in educational settings. A central theme interwoven through all of these norms for action is that the teaching/learning process is essentially a *human* undertaking. These norms are doubly important in online learning environments in which f2f interactions are mediated by technology. We have maintained in this section that the intellectual part of learning is promoted when learners' psycho-social-emotional needs are met. This relationship between feelings and thinking shows that the instructor must consider emotional and cognitive factors equally.[16]

Ethical and Professional Considerations

Closely aligned with the development of a positive work environment is the realm of professional ethics.[17] The following condensed grouping of essential ethical qualities synthesize what most educators believe should guide the professional conduct of teaching personnel at the post-secondary level.

Most post-secondary institutions have established formal policies in sub-sections of their collective agreements that delineate expectations for the professional conduct of their faculty members, whether they conduct f2f or virtual courses. These documents often identify ethical principles of professional responsibility in three areas: commitment to students, to colleagues, and to the institution. These statements serve as guidelines for professors' behaviour in their teaching role.[18]

How can online instructors demonstrate ethical standards?

Commitment to Students

Faculty members should assist all students to reach their potential in learning. They do so by applying their knowledge and skills in the content of the subject, the generic skills of teaching, TPACK, and the respectful treatment of students.

Commitment to Colleagues

Faculty members should cooperate with their peers in pursuing the common goal of promoting student learning. They fulfill their ethical obligation to resolve any professional or personal disagreement with a colleague in private. If an instructor believes that a colleague has acted unethically in a matter, he/she first discusses it with that person before reporting the situation to his/her supervisors.

Commitment to the Institution

Instructors should adhere to the policies of the employing institution with regard to teaching, research, and public service. They avoid conflicts of interest, and they ensure that the institution's procedures and regulations are followed regarding both the students' and their own academic work.

However, some educators assert that abiding by any type of procedure that might restrict their academic freedom smacks of indoctrination, compulsion, forced "character repair," or even sectarianism;[19] and that such inducement to conformity should have no place in a university. Yet, we believe that these three above commitments merely promote desirable moral and ethical principles that all post-secondary teachers should follow.[20] In our view, these actions will (a) *directly* help to produce a positive learning-teaching atmosphere and (b) *indirectly* help to satisfy the growing societal demand for college graduates who exhibit principled ethical conduct.[21]

The Managerial Process: Organizational Routines and Strategies

The managerial process is defined as what the instructor says and does – outside of the strictly instructional portion – to create the conditions conducive for teaching/learning to take place.[22] For reflective and analytical purposes, we have categorized this classroom management and procedural component into two segments: (a) What successful instructors do to motivate learners prior to and at the beginning of a course and (b) What they do during and after the course to maintain this motivation.

Although classroom management and procedural routines may seem trivial, research has revealed that this area of teaching is critically important.[23] Findings show that: students expect their instructors to exercise management and control; new instructors are initially more concerned about content than about management – until after they begin teaching; and effective management produces these positive results (e.g., minimizes disruption, enhances task engagement, maintains learning momentum, and maximizes learning).

What unique elements do online teachers plan for?

In actual practice both the management and instructional components of the teaching/learning process occur simultaneously, but we have separated these two domains and analyzed them in terms both of research findings and of our personal experiences in a variety of educational settings.

Management before a Course Begins

The literature[24] suggests that skilled instructors at all levels and in all subjects, plan, prepare, and organize their teaching prior to the first meeting of a course. They not only sense a moral obligation to enhance students' learning, but they desire to develop and/or improve their own professional skills.[25]

Planning for Procedures and Routines.[26] Prior to the first class meeting, successful teachers will have thoughtfully prepared for the administrative arrangements, facilities, technologies, policies, rules, and routines that will facilitate the smooth operation of the class proceedings.

The setting.[27] For f2f courses instructors will have examined the ventilation/lighting, availability of computers and data projectors, access to areas for group work, and overall comfort level of the setting. For virtual settings, instructors will ensure that all students will have access to the internet (via personal user name and password designations), to the online course material, to necessary equipment, and to ongoing support both for the content and technical aspects.

Administrative routines.[28] Although many of these procedural matters may seem of minor importance, effective teachers realize that, if neglected, these seemingly insignificant details could lead to frustrations, delays, student inattention, escalation of confusion, and dissatisfaction. Routines such as accessing/ distributing materials, making transitions from whole-group to small-group tasks, using online communication tools for interactive discussion, and consistently abiding by accepted social conventions for contributing to discussions or answering questions will all have been clearly conveyed and explained to students ahead of time.

Expectations.[29] When planning expectations and procedures, good instructors anticipate the typical behaviours and responses of learners with whom they are working. They also consider the institutional policies and regulations that pertain to student deportment on campus, as they formulate, beforehand, a basic set of ground rules that will apply to their particular learning setting.

Positive communication.[30] Another element in planning a core set of course expectations is that expert instructors tend to accentuate the positive rather than the negative aspect of learner conduct, thus conforming with the goal of applying ethical principles to help create an inviting socio-emotional learning climate. Moreover, proficient instructors will prepare a sound rationale for the expectations.[31] Instructors of online courses will implement a formal *acceptable use policy* (AUP) to communicate expectations for electronic communication.

**TIP
Plan beforehand how to deal with cheating.**

Alignment with institutional policies.[32] When effective instructors pre-establish their own course procedures they will have considered the institution's policies and regulations concerning student conduct with respect to the area of academic honesty.

Questions of cheating (i.e., the giving or receiving of any unauthorized assistance or unfair advantage in any form of academic work), plagiarism (i.e., the copying of the language, structure, or idea of someone else and claiming or attempting to imply that it is one's own work), falsification (i.e., any type of forgery, tampering, adding, deleting, changing of any academic documentation, or unauthorized accessing of another's computer files), or academic sabotage (i.e., any purposeful vandalism, tampering, theft, destruction of any academic equipment or materials) are usually addressed in the institution's code of honour, academic calendar, or other public documents.

The onus is on students to comply with these standards; however, some of them may not have even realized that such codes exist, let alone to have previously read or considered them. The ease with which cheating can occur is attributable in part to the voluminous amount of easily accessible information available on the World Wide Web. For instance, a sample web search will often identify a selection of papers and related documents connected to a student's assigned topic.

In fact, cheating by students in higher education[33] has increased, both in exam situations (e.g., using mobile electronic devices to copy, help others cheat, or make/pass crib notes), and in other recorded work (e.g., ignoring footnoting, submitting work done by another, collaborating on work – all without authorization).

All instructors experience their share of these incidents, but on the basis of their desire to build a cooperative learning atmosphere, we hope that they will have pre-established and posted a set of policies that reflect their ethical standard: to treat all students as if they desire to do right. However, if certain students choose not to do so, effective instructors will have also anticipated how to handle the cases that inevitably arise regarding these matters.

Management at the Beginning of a Course

Establishing Procedures. How do exemplary instructors introduce and implement these procedures during the first few class meetings? It is easier to present one's expectations prior to the first day, and subsequently to deal with any issues, than it is to wait and let them escalate into major problems.[34]

The first session.[35] It is wise to have pre-established key procedures, because first impressions are critical. Instructors want to appear organized, prepared, and well aware of university life. They will complete three tasks prior to the first day: (a) they introduce themselves and the students, (b) they describe the course –its objectives, key topics, evaluation process, and basic expectations, and (c) they begin work. With respect to on-line courses, instructors will have posted the course outline and perhaps an introductory video, which also invites (or requires) students to post an introduction of themselves. Many instructors also use an initial (but brief) "icebreaking" activity with the group to help establish a positive atmosphere.

Instructional "presence" is created by constant attention to engaging learners.

The first few days.[36] Exemplary instructors are able to balance a confident, business-like style with a positive non-threatening manner.[37] These qualities are not mutually exclusive and by demonstrating them, instructors reflect the fundamental ethical norms described earlier (i.e., a humane attitude, respect, honesty, and fairness), while at the same time implementing the management procedures in a consistent and reasonable manner. That is, they are serious about the tasks yet are supportive and encouraging. In doing so, these instructors quickly learn and use students' names,[38] which in itself is a powerful management tool.

During this critical implementation period, teachers utilize structure and motivating learning activities and they continue to monitor student progress and conduct, providing timely and diplomatic feedback. During the first few sessions, good instructors constantly monitor student and group action and inaction: they are efficient at observing, monitoring, providing necessary assistance, questioning, probing, praising, and correcting as the situation warrants. In online settings, they observe and reply to all students' web postings, they keep track of their records of accessing course materials, and they assess their individual achievement. If required, instructors may have to review or re-teach an expectation with the entire group, or with small groups or individuals.

A fundamental principle underlying all of these managerial activities and interventions is the instructor's desire to create a positive and productive course community.

Establishing a Collegial Atmosphere.[39] Skilled instructors know the importance of establishing a collegial working environment. Successful teachers are perceived as competent, confident, and knowledgeable (on the instructional side), and as pleasant, fair, and honest (on the human relations side). Combining these traits is essential for instructors who wish to create a welcoming and collaborative environment. Specific actions that they take to establish this climate are described below.

Assertiveness.[40] Effective instructors tend to project a confident and assertive manner, and by doing so they are able to sidestep being either aggressive or non-assertive.[41] Assertive instructors emphasize a balanced consideration of all sides in a conflict so "I win and you win." They seek a mutually supported solution to relationship problems, in which teachers directly present their position but also understand the others' stance.

Presence.[42] Ways that exemplary teachers project confidence and "presence" is that they communicate with conviction and enthusiasm, and interact without appearing to be arrogant or rude. They convey their expectation that everyone will attend to the activity at hand. To create presence in both f2f and online settings, skilled instructors use appropriate timing, pacing, and momentum in such a way that motivates learners in the task at hand.[43] They also pay continual attention to students' reactions, and are able to adapt their responses almost immediately to help maintain learners' high levels of engagement. Despite instructors' different personality types and styles, they can learn new and/or refine present skills that will help to create interest and motivation, both for themselves and among students.[44]

In f2f situations, effective instructors incorporate the following strategies to help raise learning motivation levels:[45] (a) by using *mobility* or breaking "the invisible six-foot leash" that typically holds traditional presenters at the front of a classroom, and by casually moving about the room; (b) using their *voice* by varying their pacing, pitch, volume, tone, modulation and projection as the situation warrants; (c) *pausing* appropriately, to add dramatic effect, stress the importance of a statement, or provide time for students to think, attract attention, make transitions, or promote expectancy; and (d) *gesturing* to focus learners' attention on key concepts in a lecture, or to point to certain items on a visual. Online instructors may use adaptations of the above strategies, but they will also ensure that they are regularly available to students for online consultation and clarification.

In this section we summarized how effective instructors initiate procedures during the early portions of a course, and how they attempt to create a both a positive and productive work climate. In the next section we seek to answer the question, "How do they sustain the process, once it has been established, for the remainder of the course?"

Maintaining the Positive Atmosphere

Provide Feedback.[46] Effective instructors not only initially establish a co-operative learning environment, but they are proficient at maintaining the productive climate throughout the course. To do so they continually monitor the activities and students' responses to the various events and tasks, and they are quick to provide genuine feedback and reinforce student success and growth.

Key positive actions that successful instructors apply during teaching/learning activities are: genuine praise, smiles, nods, and gestures. The negative responses are few and far between: using sarcasm, frowns, negative facial expressions and body language. The emphasis is on maintaining the positive community climate, providing constructive feedback that encourages development, and sustaining the intergroup trust that had been established.

When learners first begin to practice a new learning task, they require positive feedback for what they do correctly. Then, as they progress by succeeding at step-by-step successive approximations toward the final goal, expert instructors reinforce each improvement. However, they occasionally hold back reinforcement so that it does not become automatically expected. In these cases, learners experience needed periods of cognitive dissonance in which they are forced to struggle with a problem, and in which they must substantiate for themselves whether their proposed solution is correct and their response is defensible.

 "*Do not sidestep providing negative feedback*"

Offer Constructive Criticism.[47] Successful instructors do not ignore providing negative feedback if students' performance requires it. Although most instructors do not relish administering aversive judgments, they occasionally must do so to maintain their professional credibility and the authenticity. However, those that do so have also developed their skill to be able to discern between responses that require intervention and those that are minor in nature.

TIP
Teaching is essentially a human enterprise.

If consequences are warranted, effective instructors are able to maintain their overall positive manner without appearing overbearing or provocative to students – and yet they are able to administer the necessary feedback objectively and judiciously in private. They seek to minimize any humiliation and embarrassment of the offenders, as demonstrated by their use of "I messages" that express the teacher's actions and perspectives, rather than using an accusatory "You did wrong." Applying a consequence of this sort preserves the integrity of the instructor through an appeal to ethical conduct on the part of both the teacher and the learner.

Respond Proactively.[48] Effective instructors emphasize preventive and proactive procedures. A major influence on successful teachers' management skills appears to be their strong commitment to the ethical teaching principles of humanness, honesty, fairness, and respect. The teachers' application of these principles in the daily routines of the course gradually generates the desired learning climate characterized by both task productivity and a positive attitude. Because such an atmosphere is present, when instructors must deal with serious discipline matters, a fundamental tone of stability and fairness seems to undergird the entire process.

Emphasize Academic Honesty.[49] Experienced faculty members emphasize academic honesty, and they provide students with resources and contacts related to ethical academic conduct. Yet, they do recognize that they must have evidence of student's academic cheating, plagiarism, or falsification before any accusations are made. Where this evidence does exist, there is a relatively straight forward process of following the institution's published procedures for dealing with these matters. The instructor initiates the process with the student, in private, and then a chain of events unfold, leading eventually to formal disciplinary action being administered by the institution.

Although these cases are sometimes unpleasant and lengthy, the ethical standards upon which academic and professional conduct are based have two goals: to build students' (and instructors') confidence and competence, but also to correct and reprimand anyone who violates the code of honour.

If a student must be confronted for academic honesty issues, experienced instructors do so assertively. They remain calm, and they present the facts in a straight forward manner. They tend to take a non-adversarial approach, and simply state what was observed and what evidence exists. One comforting point regarding the issue of academic honesty is that findings from research coincide with one of the main messages of this manual, which is that when students feel like they belong to a caring community they are less likely to cheat than if they felt socially isolated, detached, or alienated from the institutional environment.[50] Successful instructors who create a strong sense of group- and campus-community use various strategies to achieve it, such as promoting the institution's campus-wide honour code, or providing for significant student involvement in settling cases involving academic honesty.

Developing Teaching Instincts

Because teaching is essentially a human profession,[51] it is a complex often unpredictable enterprise. Some instructors may eventually withdraw from teaching for various reasons: it is not rewarded adequately, it can be chaotic, it can be difficult to do correctly, and it takes time and energy to improve one's teaching skills. However, many individuals who decide to make teaching a career excel at it.[52] They get their rewards not only from salary or promotion, but from help-

What are some other reasons teachers might withdraw from the profession?

ing learners develop their knowledge, skills, and attitudes for the future. They are able to sense when the teaching/learning process begins to get tedious for learners or for themselves, and they are able to adjust their plans accordingly. The act of sensing this issue is even more difficult when there is separation of the learner from the instructor and the physical campus environment. Online instructors must work hard to reduce the transactional distance between the online learners and themselves. Those who are most successful employ a variety of creative and stimulating activities. Moreover, they find time and expend energy to enhance their own instructional skills.

What are the key qualities of a good concept map?

SUMMARY

In this chapter we have examined how exemplary teachers apply some of the foundational principles of effective teaching and learning motivation in order to create a positive learning environment, in online and regular settings. We described how they rely on this climate as they implement their plans for designing productive procedures and routines. Effective teachers' credibility and authenticity are enhanced when they deal with people humanely, honestly, fairly, and respectfully. These norms guide the way they both plan and incorporate their course procedures. Within this productive climate they establish and maintain their strong commitment to helping students learn: their positive attitude is instrumental in increasing learning motivation.

Footnotes

[1] Bailey (2012); Edgerton (1996); Wlodkowski (2011)

[2] Gacio Harrolle (2012a, 2012b); Lindroth & Berquist (2010); Ralph (1982, 1989)

[3] Lim (1996)

[4] Lester (2009); Ramsden (2003, 2011)

[5] Brown & Groff (2011); Hoofnagle (2012); Murray (1987)

[6] Brookfield (1995, 1996, 2004); Doyle (1997, 2008); Nord (1990)

[7] Anton-Oldenburg (2002); Wise (1996)

[8] American Psychological Association (APA, 2010)

[9] Amirault & Visser (2010); Luyegu (2012)

[10] Ahluwalia & McCreary (n.d.); Coombs (2010)

[11] Baggio & Beldarrain (2011); Love & Love (1996); Weimer (1997c)

[12] Jarvis (2006); Ralph (1998); Shils (1983); Wilson & Conyers (2013)

[13] Aronson (1987); Brookfield (1996, 2006); Wlodkowski (2011)

[14] Ramsden (2003, 2011)

[15] Brookfield (1995, 1996); Ralph (1998); Truebridge (2014)

[16] Love & Love (1996); Reyes (2013a); Willis (2006)

[17] Doyle (1997, 2008); Shils (1983); Weimer (1996c)

[18] Nothing (1994)

[19] Kohn (1997)

[20] Palmer (2010)

[21] Lombardi (2008); Teo (2009)

[22] Levin et al. (2012)

[23] Kounin (1970); Ralph (1994)

[24] Columbia College (2013); Waldron & Moore (1991)

[25] Bain (2004); Reigeluth (1996)

[26] Lai (2010); Rakes & Dunn (2010)

[27] Angelov et al. (2010); King (2012); Sulla (2012)

[28] Dabbagha & Kitsantasb (2012); Stein & Wanstreet (2012)

[29] Moore (2014); Stern (2006)

[30] Notterman & Drewry (1993); Raffini (1993); Tamblyn (2006)

[31] Bates (2013b); Beckett (2013); Knapper (2004)

[32] Dalziel & Poot (2011); The surge (2013)

[33] Foster (2014); McCabe & Trevino (1996); Thirty years (1996)

[34] Gordon (2013); How the digital (2013)

[35] Lafuze (2012)

[36] Elliott et al. (2000); Ralph (1994, 1998, 2004); Snowman et al. (2012); University of Saskatchewan (2008)

[37] Nadelstern (2013)

[38] Lambert et al. (1996); Ralph (1998); Yelon (2006)

[39] Gagné & Wager (2002); Kumar (2012); The landscape (1994)

[40] Svinicki (1992)

[41] Aronson (1987); Levin et al. (2012); Ralph (1998)

[42] Filene (2005); Jackson (2011)

[43] Ralph (2004)

[44] Kraft (1990); Symtext (2010); Torrance & Myers (1973)

[45] Palloff & Pratt (2013)

[46] Harrington (2013); Pollio & Humphreys (1988); Smith (2008)

[47] Davies (2010); Lowman (1987); Wiggins (1993)

[48] Bates (2013b); Fiedor (2012)

[49] McCabe & Pavela (2000)

[50] McCabe & Trevino (1996, p. 33)

[51] Schifter (2008); Wilson & Conyers (2013)

[52] Danish (2012); Jackson (2011)

CHAPTER 3

INSTRUCTIONAL PRACTICE

KEY IDEAS

Related to the managerial aspect of effective teaching is the key component of the actual *instruction* process. It embodies not only the content of the subject matter of the course being taught, but also the pedagogical and technological dimensions. In Chapter 3 we present basic principles of effective instruction, motivation, and TPACK. This synthesis represents a summary of what we believe reflect best practices related to teaching in current post-secondary educational settings.

The organizational format we follow in Chapter 3 was illustrated in Figure 1.5. We present this information in pragmatic terms, suitable for practicing instructors who desire to apply

How can online instructors maintain pacing and momentum?

and/or adapt instructional and technological elements to motivate learners. We conceptualize instruction as the deliberate arrangement of experiences to help a learner achieve a desirable change in performance.[1]

In this chapter you will learn:
- A core principle of planning; aligning learning objectives, activities, and assessments;

The New Forums Better Teaching Series / 47

- Both short- and long-term instructional planning is essential, but must be flexible;
- Plans for lessons, modules, units, and terms have key components;
- Implementing core presenting skills promote lasting learning ;
- Implementing five key questioning skills facilitates learning;
- Learning is enhanced when instructors incorporate eight basic responding elements.

Figure 3.0. Do **all** members clearly understand **all** the procedures and directions?

Planning for Instruction[2]

We have asserted that supporting your teaching with technology can create an improved learning experience for you and your students. We have shown that the basis of good teaching includes a variety of research-backed elements that enhance learning motivation, with technology being a key component. A well-planned and well-executed application of technologies will contribute positively to your pedagogical success and to your students' learning. Although trite, the adage "To fail to plan is to plan to fail" is a truism. All

TIP

To fail to plan is to plan to fail.

effective instructors plan --both for managing class logistics and for instructional procedures. Often, for experienced instructors this planning process is almost automatic and they may have little or no written agenda. Novice teachers, on the other hand, typically lack the accumulated wisdom of teaching practice from which to draw and they thus find it useful to create written instructional plans and to follow and/or adapt them.

Rationale for Planning[3]

Successful instructors engage in planning because:
1. It enables them to prepare materials/methods/media ahead of time.
2. It gives them an opportunity to reflect on events before and after they occur in order to modify the process for the future.
3. It helps them align the learning objectives, activities, and assessment.
4. Long-range planning (by the term, month, week, or unit of work) makes planning for individual class periods much easier. Once the larger plan is complete, the single sessions can be designed more quickly than if the course was being planned only one day at a time.
5. Planning documents could also be saved by instructors for later use, such as including them in a teaching portfolio.[4]

A Core Principle[5]

Before presenting some general planning guidelines, we re-emphasize the fundamental premise that consolidates congruency among the learning *objectives*, the learning *activities/technologies*, and the learning *assessment*.

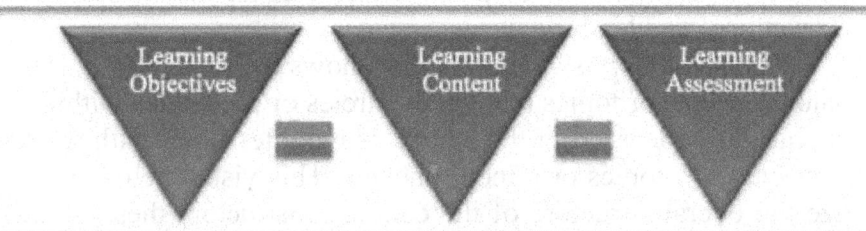

Figure 3.1: Core Principle of Planning

This principle assumes that the technology applied to help align and integrate the assessment of student learning with the session's objectives and activities is crucial. The technology is used by the instructor to connect the planning and implementation phases of instruction.

The Planning Action

Most practitioners plan in pragmatic terms, beginning with essential questions such as: "What am I supposed to cover?" "How many class periods will I have to fill?" "How can I best match these two elements?" and "What types of activities and technologies can I incorporate to enhance learner motivation?"

Instructors typically engage in planning for both the long and the short-term. We recommend that instructors new to teaching write detailed instructional plans for the first few class periods. By doing so beginning teachers will: (a) conceptualize more clearly the content and methods of each session; (b) understand how objectives, activities, and assessment fit together; (c) remember to prepare materials; and (d) have clearer direction for their instruction.

Module/Unit planning.[6] A module or unit of work relates to a specific segment of content in a course that usually takes several class periods to complete. Effective teachers carefully prepare modules or units, because it gives them a holistic vision of a single topic and allows them to extract more easily their daily lesson plans from this larger module or unit plan. A formal module plan[7] typically consists of these components: an introduction (1/2 to 1 page in length), a concept-map (1/2 to 1 page), an orientation-outline (1 or 2 pages) that presents in a few rows and columns the essential instructional components, and a bibliography.

The *introduction* summarizes the course's content, and gives the needed orientation to help instructors plan for meeting learners' instructional and learning needs.

A *concept map* is a diagram that shows the typical four or five major concepts or topics (shown by circles or rectangles within the graphic) to be learned in the course or module, along with several connected sub-topics or minor concepts. This visual helps to organize the overall structure of the content. Instructors then estimate how many class periods will be needed to teach the unit, and they place consecutive numerals beside each circle (to represent Day 1,

Day 2, etc.) according to appropriate time and coverage. Many computer applications are available to help instructors create concept maps or learning webs. The flexible nature of the software enables the instructor to graphically manipulate course themes.

Then, if the instructor so desires, he/she could further transform the concept map into a more detailed format arranged in a *columnar matrix,* consisting of rows (Day 1, Day 2 etc.) under five headings : Topic (or major concept), Instructional Objectives, Procedures/Activities, Materials/Resources, and Evaluation Strategies. For each day, instructors could summarize with bullets the key points required under each heading. A formal *bibliography* could be included at the end, listing all resources used in presenting the unit, such as: websites, URLs, curriculum guides, textbooks, media, other teachers' materials, invited guests, and so forth.

Neophyte teachers could profit from the planning experience because having to conceptualize and to articulate what and how they would arrange and implement the instructional activities and technologies would also facilitate their reflection: why they chose the particular technologies/activities; how well these elements functioned; and what might be retained, adapted, or withdrawn in the future. Moreover, they could address the following critical questions: (a) Were students motivated to learn? (b) Were instructors varying their learning activities and technologies to enhance this motivation? (c) Were the teaching/learning tasks congruent with the learning objectives? (d) Were the evaluation tasks congruent with the objectives and activities? and (e) Were instructors willing/able to adjust areas requiring it?

Lesson Planning: Because individual session plans can be extracted easily from the columnar-matrix format, we offer the following guidelines for a single period plan that consists of nine main components. This lesson or class-session plan is an overall outline of one to two pages in length. We describe a typical session plan, and also offer comments on how effective instructors actually deliver or present the session: that is, how they actually transfer the lesson from the plan to online or regular classroom practice.

1. The **Introduction** records the topic of the day, the course, and the date, time, and location.
2. The **Objectives** state precisely what students should learn or be able to do by the end of the session. For or an inquiry-

or discovery-based or open-ended lesson, in which instructors do not want to specify beforehand what students will learn, they will still state or post explicit objectives, but not pre-specifying them in terms of what "learn." See Figure 3.2 for example.

3. A **Motivational Set or Set Induction** is a short event presented at the beginning of a session to gain learners' attention or pique their curiosity, such as: a brief web video, a podcast, a puzzling statement or visual, or a short demonstration accompanied by a question. Almost anything can serve as a motivational set, and it is only limited by the imagination of the instructor.

4. The **Methods** are the pedagogical approaches or strategies that the instructor has selected to achieve the session's objectives. Effective instructors use a variety of methods to ground the experiences in the principles of learning motivation: gaining/holding learner attention, arousing curiosity, making the tasks relevant, avoiding tedium/boredom, accommodating divergent learning styles and interests, relating to real-life experience, and enhancing active learning. **Effective instructors use a variety of methods and media** Some examples of methods are: lecture, small-group tasks, online discussion, videoconference, role plays/simulations, demonstration, debates, panel discussions, laboratory investigations, talking circles, learning activity modules or packets, and independent study. The longest section of the session or lesson plan is typically the *Activities* component. It lists in chronological order what will happen during the period. In point form the instructor lists *who* does *what*, *when*, and *where*. The plan should indicate how each activity reflects the instructional objectives.

5. The **Key Questions** that instructors intend to ask or post during the session should be documented. Key questions that are posed clearly and concisely can serve as powerful motivators of student learning. Under this heading, instructors indicate only questions that refer to important concepts and that directly connect to the learning objectives. In this

way, teachers again ensure that their instructional goals are aligned with the actual learning experiences. The key questions may be posed at any time during the session, but most often they are either a part of the initial motivational set, or they are posed at main junctures and transition points in the session, in order to summarize major concepts or skills that learners have just studied or practiced. Research[7] on teachers' questioning indicates that it is one of the most challenging instructional tasks to master. When learners are questioned, their level of motivation increases, as compared to when they are simply "told" information.

Discussion[7] is essential in all courses to allow for free thought and reflection related to the content. Some questions may be posted to initiate an interchange of views amongst students and instructors. This early contact is especially important in online environments where only virtual opportunities exist to help course members connect with each other.

6. A **Summary**[8] is generally provided not only at the end of a class session, but at strategic points throughout the session in order to help learners synthesize what has been accomplished in each segment of learning. There are two types of summaries: teacher- and learner-initiated. The latter is preferred, because students will have to be more actively engaged in cognitively processing the material and in publicly stating/posting/defending their existing understanding of the topic. Again, student motivation is stimulated.

Summaries occur in formal presentation situations, in online sessions, or after small group work and discussions to help distill both what has been, and what may still need to be learned. Students learn more effectively when instructors ensure that summaries are scheduled *both* during *and* at the end of a session.

On their lesson or session plans, instructors may write brief statements as to where and what the summary will be, and they verify that these summary statements are congruent with the learning objectives (as well as with the key questions, *and* with the learning activities employed in the class-session). Examples of such summaries might be: writing a short memo to the instructor sharing what the student has learned, or posting a message to the course discussion board, blog, or wiki that shares a learner's thoughts about the session.

 Summaries may also indicate what still needs to be learned.

---

7. The **Assessment**[9] or evaluation segment of the session plan is a specific task, event, or activity that instructors incorporate to determine if the learning objectives have in fact been achieved. With formal assessments in particular, students would have been previously informed of the task and how it was to be evaluated/graded.

    Evaluation could also be informal in that the instructor may not award specific course-credit for a task, but he/she would be vigilant in observing (and noting) students' work, performance, demeanor, or sense of group cooperation. Instructors could provide feedback to students about these elements in order to assist the latter in ultimately developing their own self-assessment skills. The evaluation component could also be classified as either *formative* (i.e., ongoing, continual, or periodic – and often informal – throughout the term to show learners how they are developing or being "formed") or *summative* (i.e., more formal tasks that evaluate students' progress at the end of a unit or a term: a "sum" of their achievement).[10]

    Whatever assessment method is employed, effective instructors are aware that evaluation is not separated from but integrated into the learning experiences. By being creative in devising different assessment tasks, instructors can add to the motivation already inherent in the process.[11]

8. The **Materials** and online resources needed during the sessions are all listed on the session plan. Teachers show forethought by having all equipment, handouts, web links, and other required resources ready for the session. As they plan and prepare these resources, effective teachers se-

lect them on the basis of their instructional relevance to the lesson. Occasionally, unforeseen events may occur that cause distractions for instructors and students alike. Effective instructors anticipate such possibilities, and prepare contingency strategies for such events as: power outages, missing passwords, unreliable Internet connections, booking conflicts, time-zone differences, or other unforeseen surprises.

Other planning formats.[12] Instructors may use other methods by which to plan their coursework as well. For instance, some may plan weekly or bi-weekly agendas depending on the number of times they meet their classes within the institutional timetable. Others may plan via tri-weekly, monthly, or whole term formats. In such agendas, experienced instructors tend to record only broad outlines of main topics with brief but specific notations for using particular activities, media, materials, or personnel, as applicable. Beginning teachers appear to benefit initially from conceptualizing their plans in fairly detailed steps, and then gradually reducing the amount of detail as they become accustomed to the process.

We have presented the above information for planning individual class-periods and longer modules to provide a framework of how novice instructors often prepare for teaching. We offer it for those who may be instructing for the first time, and also for those more seasoned practitioners who may wish to reflect on the effectiveness of their instructional planning.

Implementing Instruction

Although instructional planning is essential, the ultimate goal is to implement the proposed activities and technologies in the live action of the actual teaching/learning setting. We thus provide instructional personnel with practical implementation strategies for three generic teaching methods that integrate motivational principles and technologies. We present the three generic skill sets separately, but in reality, they often overlap and are combined according to the unique contexts of each situation.[13]

Help learners understand why a response may be incorrect.

Moreover, competent instructors virtually apply these skills all the time, regardless of the specific teaching method, learning activity, and technology they may be incorporating in a particular class session. The skill sets can be described as: (a) presenting (i.e., structuring the format of activities); (b) questioning (i.e., posing/posting key questions to guide learning); and (c) responding (i.e., interacting with learners).

> **TIP**
> Three essential instructional skill-sets are Presenting, Questioning, and Responding

Presenting

A key characteristic of exemplary instructors is that they communicate their message a clearly whether they are presenting in an f2f format or facilitating an online discussion. These instructors structure the teaching/learning experiences in such a way that all participants know exactly what is expected of them, yet the teachers have learned to be flexible, open, and inviting in conducting their interactions.

Ten specific sub-skills have been identified by several researchers[14] as key practices for effective presenting of content, as described below.

1. Clarity.[15] Effective instructors are characterized by their ability to communicate clearly and concisely, which is especially important in online learning environments due to the absence of face-to-face interaction, gestures, facial expressions, and body language. Transactional distance refers to the impact on the learner and instructor based on the distance that separates them during the learning process. Therefore online participants are regularly encouraged to request clarification whenever required.

Effective instructors are careful to model clear language in online and f2f course interactions. They avoid vagueness, ambiguity, redundancy, verbal mazes, false starts, halts in speech, tangles of words, unessential content, annoying verbal mannerisms, and filler words/expressions. They often present their subject matter by (a) chunking a sequenced series of steps or segments in order to maximize student learning; and (b) incorporating appropriate video, animation, or audio resources to elucidate newly defined terms or to connect to learners' prior knowledge.

Both the literature and teachers' instructional experiences have indicated[16] that students not only express satisfaction with classes whose professors exemplify instructional clarity, but that these students in such classes demonstrate better understanding, higher achievement, and more consistent work habits. Apparently, instructor clarity helps to reduce classroom tedium, anxiety, and uneasiness among students.

2. Pacing.[17] Pacing means arranging learning events to occur in a logical sequence and at an appropriate tempo with which students soon become accustomed and which helps expedite a smooth flow of activities. At the same time, however, instructors are able to change the focus of the routines at appropriate junctures by interspersing a variety of experiences, all of which enhances student motivation to learn. Nevertheless, in online learning courses especially, constant review of technical and instructional procedures is often necessary to maintain appropriate momentum for all members.

3. Involvement.[18] Another presenting skill is the encouragement of participants to maintain active involvement in learning activities. Effective instructors ensure that students are engaged and that they experience relevant and meaningful learning activities. In online courses, the integration of blogs, wikis, and discussion boards enhances learner motivation and engagement.

4. Engagement.[19] Effective instructors are skilled at gaining and maintaining learners' attention in the task at hand by their integration of a variety of techniques and technologies. Using a motivational set at the beginning of a session engages learners (e.g., a brief demonstration, simple question, short anecdote, catchy podcast or video clip, or short problem posed on the interactive whiteboard). For example, in an online nursing course the instructor could show a clip (prefaced with a comment such as "Carefully observe the Nurse Practitioner's hands") demonstrating a medical procedure related to the content covered in that session. Then later during the session, the instructor would deliberately refer back to this motivational set to connect the activities with the initial objectives, thereby increasing learner engagement.

5. Flow.[20] Proficient instructors ensure that the learning activities are organized, sequenced, and presented with momentum in logical segments, so that learners are able to understand, practice, and assimilate the content. In doing so, effective instructors frequently employ one or more of the following techniques: (a) emailing or posting advance organizers before each session to inform students of the planned agenda; (b) posting concept maps that explain in diagrammatic form the major ideas and how they relate to each other; (c) utilizing specific descriptions/media to bridge the gap between students' prior knowledge and new learning; and (d) helping learners construct new knowledge by moving from theoretical to practical or concrete to abstract thought.

With an ever-increasing array of digital resources available to instructors, the possibilities for accommodating technology-enriched learning are numerous. Mobile learning devices[21] allow students to access course material easily from any location. Instructors who capitalize on this increased accessibility can structure their courses for maximum student engagement. By using and/or adapting a variety of instructional materials, methods, and media, they not only add interest and novelty to their content, but it helps the instructor cater to the range of students' divergent learning styles. This incorporation of instructional variety is positively correlated with higher levels of student attention, involvement, and achievement.

6. Enthusiasm.[22] Effective instructors convey that they are both *interested* and *interesting*, with respect to the subject matter they teach. A traditionally held truism about the profession of teaching is that "teachers are actors," and that their professional abilities often include their capacity to demonstrate enthusiasm, even on an occasional "off day" when they may not be particularly inclined to do so. In our view, such a role play would not be in contradiction with the ethical principles of being genuine and authentic, but it would emphasize the fact that instructors are professional. They are capable of placing the learning needs and interests of their students ahead of their own feelings. There are at least five ways that instructors can show enthusiasm and consequently invoke it in others, both in f2f and online settings:

1. by using their **voice** to help attract and hold students' attention. We have observed in our professional work, both in undergraduate/graduate teacher education (from pre-K to college-age levels) and in instructional development programs (for post-secondary levels), effective teachers in f2f settings, or in online sessions where their speech is

transmitted electronically, vocalize strategically to help create and maintain enthusiasm. They do so by varying the pitch, volume, projection, tone, and speed of their speech; by singing/rapping/chanting alone or with a group; and by vocalizing certain sound effects themselves or by leading learners in the exercise.
2. by incorporating deliberate **pauses** in their presentations in order to draw immediate learner attention, create interest, arrest inattention, increase expectancy, indicate a transition, or provide reflective time.
3. by **focusing** learners' attention by incorporating such actions as:
    - **calling** students' attention to specific objects, visuals, or concepts through verbal or non-verbal signals, or both. Examples are: "Look here;" "Are you watching?" This point is a very important;" "You will really need to remember this item;" or highlighting with color a part of a graph on the screen while stating: "Look. These two lines are distinctly different! Why?"
    - **making** gestures such as pointing to a section of a diagram, tapping one's finger on a chart, extending the hand to a portion of a map, deliberately looking and nodding in a certain direction, or combining several such gestures.
4. by **responding** quickly to student questions/comments in online settings. Furthermore, using language that conveys positive and supportive feedback for students' contributions will increase the level of acceptance, comfort, and enthusiasm perceived by the learner.
5. by **moving** around the room in f2f settings, instructors will raise the general enthusiasm level of the group because they will be able to monitor student work more accurately, maintain members' attention, and help promote more of a whole-group climate by having closer proximity to all parts of the room.

 "Instructors use five strategies to create enthusiasm"

7. Transitions.[23] Effective instructors enact clear transitions from one segment of a session to another. For instance, they indicate these shifts by stating: "That part completes the first section. Now we will advance to viewing the video clip;" "Let's summarize what we have learned in the last problem;" or "Moving on to the next number". Although veteran instructors make such transitions almost effortlessly, beginners often have difficulty in clearly and consistently articulating them because they assume that learners see and understand the material in the same way they do.

8. Verifying.[24] Effective instructors periodically check for student understanding by posing questions or by observing students applying/practicing the material. Practice alone, although essential for learning new skills, is insufficient. Feedback and reinforcement regarding one's performance are also required to solidify learning.

As learners practice performing the sub-skills of the new subject matter content, or applying their recently acquired knowledge in new situations instructors assess their performance and provide appropriate feedback on the learners' progress. This early reinforcement is often given in brief portions, and the goal is to enhance students' retention and transfer of the fresh knowledge to novel applications.

Questioning[25]

Questioning is the second generic instructional skill-set that effective instructors have mastered in online and f2f settings alike. Ever since Socrates' day, questioning has been one of the most widespread techniques of teaching; however, it also tends to be one of the most difficult teaching competencies to develop. These questioning skills are not internalized automatically into one's teaching repertoire; instructors must learn and practice them in order to make them a part of their natural teaching behaviour.

Reasons for posing questions are: to ascertain the level of students' understanding, to evaluate learning progress, to encourage learner reflection, to help instructors plan future classes/courses, to facilitate class management, and to involve students in the learning process.

Key questioning competencies[26]

A conceptual framework that has useful over the past two decades for designing questions consists of a set of five key questioning sub-skills.

1. Ascertain understanding.[27] Effective instructors pose questions to determine the level of students' understanding of specific subjects, and they tend to pose these questions at three stages in order to evaluate learning: at the beginning of a course or session, at key intervals during the learning event, and at the end of a session.

2. Ask clear, succinct questions.[28] Effective teachers who are proficient in questioning attempt to pose questions that are lucid. They avoid six common pattern errors:

- Indefinite questions (e.g., "How about motivation?") Indefinite questions are ambiguous, and often begin with "What about?" They should be re-phrased, such as, "Why do questions motivate students?"
- Multiple questions (e.g., "What are the six questioning errors? That is, define them. What are some examples? To correct a multiple question, instructors should ask each question separately.)
- Interrupted questions (e.g., "How can teachers – if it were possible and feasible – how could they really improve – that is, it would take time and dedication to do so – but how could they improve their questioning skills? Of course they must want to do so..., but anyway how would?" Such run-on questions could be corrected by having the questioner remove all the intervening fillers, and simply ask a concise question.)
- "Yes/no" type questions. Instructors who pose too many questions requiring either a "Yes" or "No" response run several risks, such as: simple guessing by students, "chorus-type" answers where no particular respondent is identified or held accountable for an answer, and where several students simultaneously call out responses, and wasting extra time by requiring increased teacher talk to ask follow-up questions such as, "Why or why not?" Many "yes/no" type questions begin with words like, "Can anyone tell me...?" or "Is (Are) there...?" or "Does anyone...?" or "Can you...?" Yes/No questions are easily reworded to require

respondents to think before answering, such as "Why do you think...?"
- Rhetorical questions. This type is often posed when no answer is expected or desired, or if the questioner intends to provide the answer him/herself. Simply waiting for someone else to answer is how such questions could be improved.

We emphasize that the overall *pattern* of these negative questions in f2f settings is what causes problems, not whether an instructor poses one or two of them.

3. Incorporate high- and low-order questions.[29] Effective instructors ask questions that require various levels of thinking. Research[30] indicates that most post-secondary instructors tend to ask many more low-order questions (i.e., knowledge level, recall, and convergent types [requiring a quick, single correct answer] than the high-order types [requiring deeper thinking]). However, skilled questioners consciously blend both types, according to the particular situation.

They realize that posing higher level and divergent questions (permitting a variety of appropriate answers) has several positive results:[31] (a) it encourages learners' reflective thinking, (b) it promotes creative and critical thinking, (c) it leads to increased student understanding and higher student achievement, (d) it yields a higher number of student responses and statements, and (e) it correlates with students' positive evaluations of the teaching they experienced.

4. Use directed questioning accompanied by adequate wait-time.[32] The effectiveness of this sub-skill appears to directly influence the effectiveness of the other four questioning competencies identified.

What are the recommended visual qualities of a slide?

In f2f instruction, a directed question is a question posed by the instructor to the entire group, followed by a pause of three to five seconds wait-time, after which the teacher designates a specific student to answer. In online learning environments, the instructor can direct a question using email, a posting, or a direct message. Wait-time will be longer and indicated beforehand. For example, the online instructor might indicate, "Here are the questions. You have three minutes to generate responses. Three minutes later the instructor will select students to respond."

Benefits of using directed questions with adequate wait-time are that: (a) learners will give longer responses, (b) they will respond more often, (c) they will begin to pose more questions, themselves, (d) they will be more actively involved in the class proceedings, (e) they will show an increase in their reasoning abilities, (f) they will be more likely to venture a response, (g) they will respond with more appropriate answers (rather than, "I'm not sure..."), (h) they will display more confidence in both the content and the process of the answering process, and (i) they will typically respond from a higher level of cognition.

We re-emphasize that in effective questioning: (a) the degree of effectiveness is determined by *the overall pattern* of questions, not isolated cases or occasional errors, and (b) the directed questioning procedure needs to be adapted and applied appropriately to one's unique context.

5. Distribute questions.[33] Effective instructors select volunteers and non-volunteers to answer, and do not permit any one student or group to dominate. The effectiveness of using directed questions, with appropriate wait-time, permits instructors to allocate questions equitably to the entire group, and they will ensure that everyone will have an opportunity to contribute to the discussion.

Reticent students may not participate unless instructors facilitate their involvement. In keeping with the basic tenets of their ethical and professional values, effective instructors are sensitive to student's feelings, carefully balancing the need to challenge students' existing thinking with their need for constructive feedback, reinforcement, and acceptance. In asynchronous online courses all students can respond at their own pace. This strategy prevents more active students from dominating the online discussion.

Responding[34]

The third skill set in which effective instructors are proficient entails responding to students. This competency is closely integrated with questioning. How an instructor typically reacts to learners' contributions often determines the ultimate effectiveness of the entire teaching/learning process.

The literature[35] has identified the importance of teacher response to students in promoting learning, because individuals' improved functioning in any area will not occur unless they receive some type of information about their progress from their mentor, coach, teacher, overseer, or supervisor. Providing an effective response is especially important with online students, who may feel isolated in their courses. Online instructors with a high degree of social presence have been found to be viewed positively by their students.

A group of colleagues in the institution where we work have developed a set of eight basic responding sub-skills,[36] which are based both on a review of the research literature from the field and upon several years of accumulated teaching and mentorship experience. We have found that effective instructor response includes the elements summarized below.

1. Recognize learners.[37] Effective instructors ground their responding actions upon the key premise that every individual is unique, worthwhile, and to be respected. By conveying this humane attitude of acceptance and by creating a learning environment where group members have their affiliation and belonging needs satisfied, effective instructors are also able to establish a reciprocal arrangement where they, themselves, gain the respect of the group members.

Research[38] on post-secondary students' evaluations of their professors showed that their ratings on five criteria were lower for instructors who made negative or threatening desists and reprimands, compared to their higher ratings for teachers who used supportive or constructive critiques. These five criteria were: instructor's competence, authority, fairness, likability, and openness to communicate with students.

2. Support students.[39] Effective instructors provide varied forms of reinforcement and encouragement to reward individuals for demonstrating achievement and effort. During course discussions, for instance, instructors may ask students for clarification, elaboration, or reaction to previous comments; and they would do so because they desire to encourage learners' creative and critical thinking. In such cases, they may pose additional provocative or hypothetical questions to stimulate this process, such as: "Does today's television programming lead to violence among young viewers?" or "How do fish communicate?" or "How would one go about finding these answers?" When students offer answers to these questions, instructors will acknowledge participants' input.

3. Delve deeper.[40] Effective teachers reinforce appropriately the correct portion of a participant's response, but also solicit more information from respondents to help them elaborate or correct any inaccurate thinking. This task requires tact and skill, but exemplary instructors perform it smoothly by delving further with a follow-up question.

In all of these probing activities successful instructors are mindful of preserving students' dignity, challenging their ideas, requesting them to substantiate their claims, asking for more evidence for an assertion, or soliciting defensible arguments for their position. At the same time, a quality of effective instructors is that while enacting these probes they sidestep emphasizing negative criticism or disdain.

When instructors help students address cognitive dissonance that may arise from processing the material, the latter will develop advanced levels of thinking. The research[41] on the instructional practice of probing sensitively has confirmed that it: (a) is associated with higher measures of student achievement; (b) it leads to increased quality and quantity of student involvement; (c) it reduces the frequency of non-responding by students; (d) it leads to higher level responses from members; and (e) it helps respondents (and on-looking non-respondents) to attempt to provide more clarity and detail in subsequent answers. In like fashion, online instructors will similarly respond to a student's post in order to generate further insight and to model interaction strategies for other students.

4. Respond courteously. Some educators[42] believe that when a student's response is incorrect, the instructor should reject the answer with a statement like, "No! That is incorrect!" To do less, they suggest, may convey that the instructor is weak or afraid to be assertive, or may make the student feel uncertain as to the correctness of his/her response. However, other educators[43] advocate refraining from being so blunt, but rather to couch the rejection of the answer in milder terms, such as, "You're on the right track..." or "Not quite" or "Try again."

The most sensible solution to this difference is for the instructor to be prepared to use both approaches depending to the situation and the personality of the respondent. For instance, individuals who have a positive self-image or who are extraverted and confident may profit from being told "No, that is wrong." However, such students also deserve to know why their response is incorrect, and effective instructors, online or f2f, would follow up such a statement with an explanation, a simpler re-phrased question, or a request to another student to "Help us out here." Using these less abrupt responses will not discourage the respondent (or other students observing the exchange) from attempting to contribute in the future.

5. Refrain from parroting.[44] Effective instructors in f2f and synchronous settings do not fall into the trap of echoing student responses. They habitually use other forms of reinforcement without repeating, verbatim, what students have stated. Many teachers, however, parrot learners' responses unthinkingly and immediately after students respond. If this repetition happens consistently, students tend not to listen to their peers' contributions because they realize that the teacher will repeat the answers on "instant playback." Hence, a sort of sub-conscious dependency on the instructor is reinforced, while the opportunity for encouraging student-to-student interaction is nullified because of the instructors' unconscious but constant echoing of students' responses.

6. Observe other cues.[45] Experienced instructors in f2f settings are not only skilled at reacting to learners' oral and written responses, but they show sensitivity to their non-verbal cues as well. Just as instructors realize the power of their own body language in either strengthening or weakening the effect of their response behaviours upon students, so they also become increasingly aware of students' facial expressions, grimaces, frowns, gestures, body posture, and other non-verbal clues, which often signal how learners are reacting. In online settings, instructors must monitor student interaction even more closely, because technology removes or diminishes non-verbal communication cues. Examples of these types of responses online might be typing in full capitals or in using inappropriate language.

7. Attend to student input.[46] Effective instructors in online and f2f courses pay attention to students' responses and suggestions. An example of this skill would be use of an interactive whiteboard between two sites. Students would post or share ideas on the whiteboard, which all participants could view and to which they could respond. Some of these responses could be: (a) reinforcing correct answers, (b) probing to help learners improve incomplete or partially correct responses, (c) inviting elaborations or clarifications, (d) requesting other students to react to the answer, (e) paraphrasing a student's comment, (f) seeking reasons why a student has expressed a certain point, (g) demonstrating empathy (e.g., "I felt that way, too, when I first read it...") We note that the instructors' interest must be perceived as genuine and not as representing artificial reinforcement, in that instructors cannot be seen as trying to be patronizing or "over sweet."[47]

8. Promote student interchange.[48] During group discussions, effective instructors encourage learners to respond to their peers' questions or comments. They are also proficient at facilitating student-to-student communication in which students interact with each other concerning the subject in question. This skill is critical for successful online learning. Students in web-based courses must interact with their instructor and with each other to fully develop an online community and to reinforce their learning.

In these cases, the students become the focus of attention, and the instructor's role changes to one of resource person or occasional guide. The instructors continue to encourage students to pose questions as a response to earlier threads. In this way students begin to enhance their own listening skills and logical reasoning abilities by devising questions for and probing their peers for clarification and elaboration of their ideas.

 "Students in web-based courses must interact to fully develop an online community and to reinforce their learning."

SUMMARY

In this section we reviewed the three generic instructional skill sets of presenting, questioning, and responding. We described how effective instructors typically implement the respective sets of sub-skills from each of these categories within f2f and online environments. The ultimate purpose of these instructional competencies is to enhance students' motivation to learn the required body of knowledge and skills related to the course(s) in question.

Footnotes

[1] Bergstrom (2011); Bloom et al. (1956); Krathwohl (2002)

[2] Fullan (2012); Heller & Procter (2011); Lynch & Roecker (2007); Tomaszewski (2012a, 2012b)

[3] Dillon & Sternberg (1986); Knapper (2004)

[4] Adlakah & Aggarwal (2011); Boddington & Boys (2011); Hernandez-Gantes (2011); Lightner (2012)

[5] Ahedo (2011); Davis (2014); Wieling & Hofman (2010)

[6] Freiberg & Driscoll (2000); Shell & Warner (2012)

[7] Acree Walsh & Dankert Sattes (2005); Ralph (1999)

[8] Eggen & Kauchak (2012); Ralph (1998); University of Saskatchewan (2008)

[9] Herman et al. (1992); Perrone (1991); Ralph (1997a); Vanderveen (2012)

[10] Clegg & Cashin (1990); Reeves (2011); Stödberg (2012)

[11] Arter (2002); Swan et al. (2006)

[12] Bergin (2001); Tomlinson & McTighe (2006)

[13] Bates (2013a)

[14] Garmston (1994); Tierney (1999)

[15] Won Park (2012)

[16] Dembo (2013); Lambert et al. (1996); Slavin (2011)

[17] Dror (2011); Ellis Ormrod et al. (2006)

[18] Ellison & Wu (2008); Kennedy et al. (2010); McCarthy et al. (2010); Purcell et al. (2013); Spitzer (2012)

[19] Prince (2004); Salmon & Edirisingha (2008); Walls et al. (2010)

[20] Novak (2012); Shell & Warner (2012); Urtel & Fernandez (2012)

[21] Gillies (2012); Keogh (2011); Kilty (2013); Kitchenham (2011); Murray (2011); Ng & Anastopoulou (2011); Stewart & Hedberg (2011); Vogel et al. (2009)

[22] Baughman (1974)

[23] Freiberg & Driscoll (2000); Tierney (1999)

[24] King (2012); Purdue University (2012)

[25] Dillon (1983); Fusco (2012)

[26] Latham (1997)

[27] Barell (2003); Foundation for (2011)

[28] Mandernach et al. (2009)

[29] Lindsay & Davis (2013); Young (2012)

[30] Ralph (1998); Torrance & Myers (1973); Wiles & Bondi (2011)

[31] Acree Walsh et al. (2005); Gardner (1993)

[32] Barell (2003); Freiberg & Driscoll (2000); Lambert et al. (1996); Ralph (1998, 1999)

[33] McFerrin & Christensen (2013); Nandi et al. (2012)

[34] Eggen & Kauchak (2012); Tierney, 1999; Torrance & Myers (1973); Wiles & Bondi (2011)

[35] King (2012); Shi et al. (2012)

[36] University of Saskatchewan (2008)

[37] Attawatikul et al. (2013); Shannon-Karasik (2013)

[38] Garner (2006)

[39] Slavin (2011)

[40] Kilty (2013); Manning & Johnson (2011)

[41] Anderson (2011)

[42] Elliott et al. (2000); Orlich et al. (2013); Ralph (1998)

[43] Viers (2009)

[44] Barell (2003); Dillon (1983); Orlich et al. (2013); Ralph (1999); Torrance & Myers (1973); University of Saskatchewan (2008)

[45] Elliott et al. (2000)

[46] Galbraith & Jones (2010); Wohlfarth & Mitchell (2012)

[47] An & Lipscomb (2010); Du et al. (2010); Kitchenham (2011); Mann (2011)

[48] Anastasiades (2012); Banks (2012a); Conole & Culver (2010)

CHAPTER 4

MOTIVATING METHODS AND TECHNOLOGIES

KEY IDEAS

In this chapter we examine several specific methodologies and technologies that effective instructors employ to motivate learners. The organizing framework consists of two basic divisions: instructor-centered and student-centered approaches, referring to who is most actively involved in the process at the time. Under instructor-centered methods, we present motivational strategies to implement lecturing, demonstrating, and discussion. Under student-centered processes, we describe stimulating approaches and technologies to incorporate small-group work, cooperative learning, discovery/inquiry learning, debates, role play, and simulations.

In this chapter you will learn:
- Motivation is enhanced by skillfully integrating teacher- and learner-centered methods;
- Three teacher-centered approaches are lecture demonstration, and discussion;
- Six student-centered approaches are: group-work, cooperative learning, discovery/inquiry learning, debates, role play, and simulation;

- Instructors implement an approach based on its unique contextual advantages and disadvantages;
- Wise instructional decision-making is based on sound motivational principles.

Figure 4.0. To what extent can digital technologies replace live interpersonal interaction, human dialogue, and cooperative/creative thinking? See Whelan et al. (2013).

Part 1: Teacher-Centered Approaches

A teacher-centered method is a sequence of learning activities that the instructor has designed to follow a logical path.[1] We describe three popular instructor-based methods using the following structure: definition, purpose, strengths, limitations, and implementation. We also suggest a variety of techniques and technologies that have been found to motivate students.

One key point is that things may not be as they appear. For instance, just because learners seem passive during a teacher-centered presentation does not necessarily translate into a poor learning situation. Similarly, with respect to student-centered activities, instructors may appear to be doing little, and yet in such cases, more teacher preparation and monitoring of group progress is often required than for a traditional lecture or instructor demonstration.[2]

Lectures

Studies[3] have shown that lecturing is a common method of teaching at the post-secondary level and is efficient in helping learners acquire new information.

Definition.[4] A lecture is a carefully prepared oral presentation by a qualified person. It is a familiar method for transmitting information or, combined with multi-media, to show how a skill is to be performed, to demonstrate a skill or concept, or to supplement course materials.

Purpose.[5] Its purpose is to convey information efficiently and effectively, particularly if the material is not readily available elsewhere, or if it is dispersed among several sources. Lectures supported by presentation technologies serve to motivate or inspire learners, to explain or describe objects or ideas, to stimulate reflection, to promote creative and critical thinking, or to provide alternative points of view.

Strengths.[6] The lecture method has several advantages:
1. It can be updated at will to make it more current;
2. The presenter can immediately modify add to, delete from, and adjust the material as required;
3. It can incorporate a variety of presentation technologies (e.g., PowerPoint, Prezi, online video, interactive polling), presenters can be more dynamic, and their material can be more visually appealing;

TIP
Lectures supported by presentation technologies can motivate learners.

4. It can be enriched through instructor enthusiasm, dramatics, humour, warmth, and intensity;
5. It permits audience interaction, questioning/answering, discussion, and social reinforcement;
6. It is controlled by the presenter in terms of content, pacing, organization and time management; and
7. The presenter can re-explain or re-teach any ambiguous segment immediately.

Limitations.[7] As with any instructional tool, lectures may be misused or abused. When lecturing has been maligned or rejected as a method, a closer examination of the negative cases shows that instead of dismissing the approach as being deficient, a more rational explanation may be that the persons implementing it have been in error.[8] Some of these ineffective applications of the lecture are: (a) instructors may try to use lectures to change learner's values and attitudes, which is *not* as effective as the discussion method for modifying participants' attitudes; (b) teachers may present lectures that are too lengthy, disorganized, or redundant; (c) instructors may attempt to use lecturing to promote learners' thinking skills, rather than employing problem-solving, inquiry, interactive, or discovery activities; (d) teachers may believe that "covering the course" is the goal; and (e) they may insist that "teaching is telling" and "listening is learning."

Implementation

We highlight key motivational strategies and activities based on the foundational principles Identified earlier in this handbook, which successful instructors employ to enliven their lectures.

1. Structure activities.[9] Effective instructors maintain structure in their implementation of learning activities: (a) they state objectives explicitly to students early in the class-session;(b) they use a motivational set to arouse learner interest; (c) their explanations and directions are precise; (d) they make clear transitions from one segment to another; (e) the activities proceed with brisk pacing and momentum to keep participants alert; (f) they summarize (or get students to do so) during and at the end of a period; (g) they ensure that learners practice applying the newly learned concepts and skills – and, (h) they provide students with feedback and reinforcement of their progress in this practice, all while allowing resilience for spontaneous events and contextual adjustments.

Skilled instructors do more than structure their presentations; they incorporate other motivational devices and techniques to stimulate learning. The use of presentation software using tested graphic design principles creates added value for the lecture and ensures content is shared in an effective manner.

2. Create a positive atmosphere.[10] To increase learners' intrinsic motivation instructors consciously build and maintain an upbeat learning environment where students feel emotionally safe, have a sense of affiliation, and are given an opportunity to make some decisions about their learning.

Students tend to be more motivated to learn if they: (a) understand the value of the course being taught; (b) believe that it will then meet personal goals; (c) see the content connected to their personal technology preferences; and (d) have expectations to succeed at the tasks.

3. **Use contemporary technologies.**[11] Incorporating current technologies and a variety of graphic design templates is effective for adding stimulating variation. These variations will ensure that content will appeal to students' different learning styles. For example, one accepted presentation principle is that instructors should use screen colours that have high degrees of contrast and have limited text (i.e., as a guideline, not to exceed 40 words per slide). In a chemistry course a video clip from the internet demonstrating the reactions in a cola beverage when certain substances are added to the liquid would be shown to students.

4. **Teach interactively**. Experienced teachers enhance their lectures by using *interactive teaching*[12] to motivate students. Interactive teaching motivates learners to be actively involved in learning activities other than writing notes, watching the teacher, and listening to the lecture. The lecture segments are interspersed with oral question/answering episodes, pair problem-solving, short discussions, resource-based learning segments (in which pairs or small-groups use varied media provided to answer a question or resolve a problem), or brief independent study activities.

A specific example of a successful modification made to a traditional lecture is provided in the health sciences, where the instructor uses an interactive white board[13] to demonstrate knee replacement surgery. Learners are able to actively participate in a simulated procedure in a classroom setting. This experiential learning process includes performing the major tasks, from making the initial incision to the final suturing. Learners manipulate virtual instruments to perform each step of the procedure, and throughout the process they receive guidance and feedback from the computer program. In medical education, having the opportunity to interactively engage in the simulated surgery is an essential step in the authentic learning process.

5. **Challenge students**. Effective instructors *challenge students' thinking*[14] by raising controversial issues; by adding an op-

posing view; by forcing learners to analyze their own assumptions and biases; or by having them explain and defend their position on an issue (or doing the same thing, except to have them deliberately argue for the opposing position – in order to force them to experience a "contradictory" stance).

6. Arouse interest.[15] Proficient instructors enhance their presentations by stimulating interest using a variety of motivational techniques, some of which are: suspense, novelty, ambiguity, incongruity, or discovery.

Other interesting activities that effective instructors incorporate into their interactive teaching are: having students who possess a unique skill teach the skill to the group; deliberately teaching students helpful information retrieval skills (e.g., the use of mnemonic devices and memory strategies, such as the traditional "Every Good Boy Deserves Fudge" for the notes on a music staff); using familiar material when giving examples, so as to help students use what they have previously learned; and minimizing the appeal of competing motivational systems, such as rewarding group interaction and discouraging uncooperative behaviour.

> **Learning is enhanced when it is transferred to practical situations.**

7. Promote learning transfer.[16] Expert teachers are proficient at helping learners to become active in transferring the "course-acquired" knowledge to real-world situations. Experienced instructors at the undergraduate level realize that a key motivational device in their courses is to structure learning activities to represent, as much as possible, the actual conditions that prevail outside of the classroom. A major shift in educational practice is to expose students to authentic learning environments where they are able to apply theory in practical ways within a real-world setting. Internships, clinical practica, preceptorships, service learning programs, and apprenticeships are examples of programs in which prospective practitioners in the professions can actively transfer their learning to new situations. These field experience programs can be expedited by participants' use of technologies that connect students to their peers, mentors, and experts in order to broaden the learning experience.

"If a learner exhibits low competence and low confidence, the instructor reciprocates with high levels both of *task-direction* and *emotional support*."

8. Sustain motivation.[17] Instructors are not able to continually maintain high levels of cognitive stimulation with all students over extended periods of time, because human beings become temporarily satiated when their needs, drives, and motives are satisfied. If any of these stimuli become over-used and commonplace, their effectiveness diminishes. However, there are a number of ways[18] that effective teachers employ to help maintain student interest and attention.

One of these key techniques is to continue to vary the instructional stimuli through the application of digital resources. For instance, creating podcasts of course meetings allows students to revisit the learning activities at their leisure. An additional technique is to periodically introduce change-of-pace activities. An example of such an activity conducted in either f2f or online settings would be to have students take two minutes to write down their reflections about a presented concept. Then, each person shares his/her response with the entire class when called upon.[19] In an online setting a wiki or videoconference system could connect all members, and would communicate everyone's responses among the whole group. In an f2f environment using microphones would ensure that all messages would be clearly sent and received.

In the above section we have shown that skilled instructors are able to transform the traditional lecture into an interactive process that motivates students to engage in a variety of active learning experiences.

Demonstrations[20]

Definition. A second category of teacher-directed approaches– and one that could also be classified as one type of interactive lecture –is the demonstration. It is defined as an instructional method in which a learner views a real or life-like example of the skill or process to be learned.

Purpose. Its goal is for the learner to imitate a physical performance or adopt the attitudes of the person modeling a particular skill. This option has dramatically improved through the application of nuances in computer animation and simulated learning-environment technologies. A classic example from biology is the online virtual frog dissection. Successful demonstrations have these characteristics:

1. Careful preparation. To be well-prepared is essential. This pre-planning not only includes having all equipment and resources ready (and tested) ahead of time, but it is also important to have a back-up in place in the event that the proposed agenda does not proceed as anticipated. Making local copies of Internet-based resources is especially helpful. Experienced instructors are aware of potential hazards and take the necessary precautions ahead of time.

2. Appropriate activities. Effective instructors match the learning activities with the existing developmental level of the learners observing and practicing the task in question. In doing so, instructors ensure that their expectations and guidance of the students are in alignment with the learners' degree of competence and confidence in performing the particular skill. Instructors do not over-emphasize perfection in their demonstration of the skill. Rather, they separate the specific skill, task, or cognitive process into discrete and understandable steps in order for students to examine each step in successive chunks before they try performing and perfecting each step.

Moreover, expert teachers teach each sub-skill with a style that matches the particular development level of the learners in performing that task.[21] For instance, if the student is at a low development level for a specific skill set, the instructor will use a style characterized by a high degree of direction and a high degree of encouragement to compensate for the low confidence level of the learner at that stage.

Video resources that demonstrate correct technique can be utilized to model processes and outcomes. There are numerous online video clips[22] related to most subjects that illustrate proper procedures, processes, strategies, and techniques.

As the learner's level of development in performing the sub-skills progresses, the instructor synchronizes his/her leadership response with that changing level. By gradually reducing the initial amount of procedural direction and psycho-emotional support, exemplary teachers adapt or adjust their demonstration strategies to meet the developmental readiness level of the learners.

3. Sustained motivation. Whether effective instructors demonstrate performing a gymnastics maneuver in Physical Education, executing a laboratory procedure in Biochemistry, participating in a formal conversation in Spanish, or performing a blood-glucose level test in Medicine, they typically exhibit the following characteristics in their demonstrations for the purpose of keeping learners motivated: (a) they prepare and structure the presentation (according to guidelines described in earlier sections of this manual); (b) they tailor their teaching style to match the readiness level of the learners to perform that skill; (c) they define and explain any new concepts or objects; (d) they begin each stage of the demonstration by summarizing what is to be done, and then they re-explain it as they do it; (e) they perform each sub-skill slowly with exaggerated and/or deliberate movements and pertinent comments; (f) they have each participant practice the sub-skills, and they provide brief but clear feedback on each learner's performance; (g) when correcting learners' mistakes, they patiently demonstrate the correct skill again, and clearly re-explain necessary procedures.

They encourage students to make further attempts, and similarly provide feedback always being sensitive to the learners' feelings and confidence levels, and always being aware of their own manner in the coaching process.[23] Ultimately, *the* key distinctive mark of an effective demonstration is clarity.

Discussion[24]

A third sub-set of teacher-directed methods is face-to-face or online discussion. We have categorized it as a teacher-centered approach because the instructor plans, prepares, and facilitates it – although online instructors should prepare students to conduct class discussions on their own, with minimal teacher intervention.

Definition. A discussion is defined[25] as the interchange of ideas among two or more people by various means of communication. The statements or questions that are created in a discussion help participants generate an exchange of ideas related to the topic.

Purposes. Instructors incorporate discussions into their courses: to enhance students' thinking skills; to promote learners' ability to support their assertions and to defend and refute arguments logically; to examine other perspectives; and to have students construct new personal meanings through a process of co-operative inquiry.

Motivating online learners to engage in meaningful discussion is sometimes difficult, and instructors who encourage online discussion through conferencing or discussion forums must work diligently to ensure student motivation does not wane. Instructors must provide reinforcement by giving students positive and frequent replies for posting contributions. Not replying may signal to students that their input is unimportant and not worth the effort, or that instructors are not reading their responses

What four strategies promote members' online participation?

Strengths.[26] Some key strengths are that discussions: (a) provide a venue where students' views, attitudes, values, and beliefs can be publicly expressed, examined, challenged, defended, and/or modified through the social interaction process; (b) promote students' higher level cognitive thinking and (c) foster students' self-initiated and extemporaneous reasoning abilities.

Limitations.[27] Some potential problems and sensible solutions that experienced instructors have applied to resolve these problems are summarized below.

1. Discussions may deteriorate into informal chats or backchannel communication dominated by a clique of active members. The problem is eliminated if the instructor initially sets and enforces the ground rules that ensures than no individual or sub-group monopolizes the conversation, and that everyone is granted equal opportunity to contribute. Effective teachers are ever mindful to maintain an inviting group atmosphere that encourages members to interact.

2. Group members may have inadequate knowledge regarding the topic, and to deal with this situation online and f2f instructors alike may require participants, as part of the ground rules for discussion, to first have the necessary background content and group process skills from which to develop the conversation.

3. Online and f2f discussions can bog down, get sidetracked, or become irrelevant, unproductive, boring, or frustrating. But so can any other teaching method unless the instructor prepares well, especially for learners who are inexpe-

rienced in participating in discussions. In order to prevent these negative potential outcomes, proficient instructors employ several strategies.
- One strategy is to clearly connect the discussion topic to one or more of the course objectives so that participants see the reason for the activity. A second approach is to carefully explain the rationale for the ground rules (i.e., respecting the right of others to have views, and being able to criticize others' positions without attacking the people).
- Third, they begin discussion activities using short, well-structured formats, such as brainstorming with the whole class (i.e., the teacher invites everyone to contribute suggestions about a topic, and the teacher types the ideas on the screen). Ground rules here are: do not judge the ideas other than not permitting offensive or obscene comments, build on others' suggestions, and accept all suggestions in any order. Then, the instructor helps the group re-arrange the items into categories, and helps them through questioning to reach tentative conclusions about the subject. Before progressing to more advanced levels of discussion in which the teacher plays a less directive role, the early discussion experiences are purposefully designed and controlled by the instructor.

4. Undergraduate students do not typically participate in class: research[28] indicated that only about 6 per cent of class time is spent in student participation, and that approximately half of students report participating "infrequently" or "almost never"; and yet nearly 97% of students state that all classes should provide for some type of student involvement.
    - Exemplary instructors address these non-participation issues by consistently employing the following techniques: posing oral questions, asking for clarification or other student responses, accepting/praising/repeating student answers, or using students' names when posing questions or giving feedback.
    - Research[29] also showed that less than a third of under-

graduate students in f2f settings make nearly 90 per cent of classroom comments, and that most students feel that speaking up in class is most suited to those vocal individuals who tend to take the responsibility for carrying the dialogue. The majority refrains from contributing because (a) they feel their contributions may not be well structured, (b) they feel unknowledgeable in the subject field, (c) they had not done the required homework, or (d) the class is too large and they would be embarrassed.

TIP
Online instructors facilitate discussion by providing members with frequent positive

5. To conduct online and f2f group discussions properly requires much energy, and it can be intellectually exhausting and often emotionally taxing. It requires instructors to have high levels of preparation, knowledge, confidence, and patience to conduct discussions. Research[30] suggests that the majority of faculty members could give more attention to incorporating discussion-type activities in their teaching. Moreover, for individuals just beginning their teaching career, the key would be to start with a small portion that is controlled and directed, to assess its effect, and then to proceed according to the results, making adjustments as necessary.

Implementation: A Distillation of Findings[31]

In this section we summarize how exemplary instructors structure and conduct effective discussions.

1. ***Establish ground rules***. They set basic procedural guidelines for member conduct during discussion, such as: active listening, no rudeness, and logical argument.
2. ***Set clear goals***. They provide explicit objectives, instructions, and a time limit (especially for initial discussion activities).

3. ***Know when to intervene.*** Effective instructors discern when to pose a question, request an elaboration, review the group's progress, or proceed to the next point.
4. ***Handle hinderers.*** They deal with individuals who block the group's progress (e.g., ensuring that monopolizers do not dominate, dealing with irrelevant issues later, defusing hostile situations, redirecting digressions or trivialities, and encouraging quiet members to contribute).
5. ***Maintain flexibility.*** Effective instructors vary their degree of direction according to the context: they adjust their control, and sometimes permit an open discussion if the situation warrants it.

In Part 1 of this chapter, we described how effective teachers implement three common teacher-centered methods: lively lectures, distinctive demonstrations, and dynamic discussions. We illustrated how they strive to prepare and present a variety of interesting learning activities for each of these approaches in order to arouse and maintain students' motivation to learn.

In Part 2, we explore how skilled faculty members prepare and arrange several stimulating student-centered learning experiences.

Figure 4.1. Is there a danger that employing technologies might produce " collaborative independence"? Or "independent collaboration"?

Part 2: Student-Centered Approaches

Like teacher-centered approaches, student-centered methodologies are also planned and implemented by the instructor, but they are incorporated in such a manner as to permit greater student choice and ownership than is the case for the more closely controlled teacher-directed methods examined in Part 1. Moreover, effective teachers characteristically blend *both* categories into integrated, holistic sessions designed to sustain learners' interest.

Teacher-centered approaches have components of student-centered tasks in them; the latter, correspondingly, have certain teacher-directed aspects. In this section, we describe some of the ways instructors implement five recognized student-centered methods. We employ the same organizational framework used in Part 1, which provides each method's definition, purpose, strengths, and limitations, along with some of stimulating strategies and technologies.

Small Group Activities[32]

Definition and purposes. A small group activity consists of a team of learners (usually three to seven) working to accomplish a certain task. The goals to be attained typically are to: (a) examine a controversial issue and to generate a set of tentative conclusions; (b) complete a class-project, or (c) solve a problem, examine a case-study, conduct an inquiry or laboratory investigation, participate in a debate or panel, or engage in a role-play, simulation, or other group activity incorporating drama. Any categorization of these methods will produce considerable overlap between and among the various approaches.

Strengths.[33] Small-group work provides for: (a) fostering the democratic ideal of pooling individuals' talents and knowledge for the good of the collectivity; (b) enhancing individuals' social and interpersonal skills; (c) promoting problem-solving competence; (d) empowering participants with increased choice and decision-making; (e) balancing the opportunity to let participants apply their unique abilities to achieving the goal; (f) permitting the open exchange and examination of a variety of perspectives in a more informal forum; (g) increasing students' active participation; (h) providing "real-world experience" of having to engage seriously in the conflict-resolution process; and (i) increasing participants' depth of understanding of the course content.

Limitations.[33] Some deficiencies of the small-group approach are:

1. To reduce the possibility of small-group tasks becoming unproductive, effective instructors arrange for the groups to engage in specific activities guided by explicit procedures and time limits.
2. Effective instructors consistently advocate the benefits of group activities, emphasizing that some conflict is normal whenever human beings interact. They also identify practical reasons for knowing how to work in groups, such as demonstrable skills in team-inquiry processes, in interpersonal communication, and in dealing constructively with others as they seek to solve often chaotic problems.[34]
3. Critics of group work are correct when they assert that the "reality" of small group activities with undergraduates does not always match the "ideal."[35] They point out: (a) that intellectual pitfalls may often be present; and (b) that social barriers may be present. Experienced instructors do not deny or ignore such problems, but they confront these difficulties early. For instance, they seek to eradicate the intellectual problems by persisting to challenge learners to view issues from outside of their own mind set; to examine consciously their internalized assumptions; and to realize everyone must seek clarity, evidence, reasoned judgment, and understanding of alternatives.

    Skilled instructors confront the non-participation issue by: employing questioning skills, reinforcing involvement, providing continued encouragement, including minority group-members, re-arranging the groups, and modeling expected behaviour themselves. They work at not reacting negatively if a student criticizes them or their ideas. They attempt not to take criticism personally but to take it seriously.[36]

Implementation.[37] Proficient instructors employ practical procedures in organizing and implementing small group activities for the purpose of increasing students' motivation to learn.

1. The small group method has been used successfully by effective teachers in some fashion for all subjects; however, certain courses may be more or less suited for this approach.
2. Simply putting students into groups will not produce automatic success. Experienced instructors are *proactive* in designing, implementing, and monitoring procedures that will tend to prevent difficulties from emerging. First, they select motivating topics that are directly related to the course objectives. Second, they organize the activity so that participants (either in pairs, triads, or larger groups) will have the necessary background information and/or group skills to complete the required task in a fixed time frame. Third, they provide precise instructions and directions of what is to be done, how the member roles are to function, and how the process/product will be assessed. Fourth, these instructors teach the fundamental group procedures and social rules that everyone is expected to follow. Fifth, they monitor the progress of each group (and individuals in it) and provide feedback as required. Positive reinforcement is prominent, but correction is occasionally administered, is given briefly, and is delivered in an objective and non-threatening manner.

 "Experienced instructors prevent group difficulties from emerging"

Cooperative Learning (CL) [38]

Definition and purposes. Most instructors regard the CL approach as a type of small group activity in which members work together to assist one another learn or to cooperate in creating a final product. A key difference from group work in general is that cooperative/collaborative group members help each other search for and grasp the meaning of a concept, process, or event. A characteristic feature of the CL approach is the mutuality, rather than the individuality, of the goal activity: the whole group is responsible for assisting all members to learn a concept, or to perform a skill, or to create a product, based on the joint achievements of each member.

Typically consisting of four to seven members, CL groups have two basic aspects: the task dimension, and the reward dimension, in which individuals receive personal credit only if the group succeeds. Members are motivated to be responsible for their fellow members' learning.

Strengths. The majority of the findings of research on CL have been consistently favourable.[39] There tends to be an increase of group members' positive attitudes toward both the subject material and their team members, as well as an extension of learners' use of higher-order thinking skills. There is also evidence of more positive psychological well-being among participants, and of a more productive and supportive learning climate.

Limitations.[40] Reasons cited for non-constructive results are that: dominant members rule; not all students cooperate; the final result may not be useful; many students are accustomed only to individual learning; and conscientious students end up doing most of the work. Furthermore, some students see it as slowing their individual pace and interfering with their own progress; participants often do not have the necessary background to sustain intelligent discussion on a topic; there is the emergence of simple logistical problems; and it is a time-consuming exercise.

Implementation. Proponents of CL identify five essential elements for successful implementation as described here.

1. **Positive interdependence**. Individuals succeed only when all members succeed. A member's work benefits the whole group, and the whole group's product benefits the individual
2. **Individual and group accountability**. Each member has a key task to perform, and the final product is incomplete without it.
3. **Productive interaction.** Members must communicate in order to promote each individual's effectiveness by describing, explaining, questioning, discussing, defending, and assessing each other's work, and by supporting, encouraging, and assisting one another.
4. **Interpersonal and group processing skills**. Effective instructors teach and model these essential skills, and require

students to use them. Students are expected to work cooperatively, communicate clearly, employ acceptable social skills, use effective decision-making and leadership principles, and exercise conflict-management processes, as required.

5. **Content knowledge**. Participants must possess sufficient subject-matter background to engage in the discussion in question. Effective instructors must monitor each group's progress and intervene when necessary to help groups to maintain both the "task" and the "collaboration" processes. The effort is time-consuming, it requires preparation and active monitoring, and it requires perseverance.[41] In order to reduce the initial workload, some instructors start with a small project related to the course, and in which groups will be motivated and successful. Then, as participants gradually become accustomed to "the roles and rules" of the method, the teacher may increase the complexity of the task. The following example illustrates how instructors can integrate contemporary technologies into CL activities: Begin with a simple introductory activity that is not related to the online course content but is one that each CL group must successfully complete before being given the topic for the assignment. The first assignment may relate to using a wiki or discussion board. The technical skills are developed at the same time as the process skills around CL.

Debates[42]

The debate is a formal and staged presentation (oral or online) involving two teams that discuss a controversial topic issue from the pro and con positions. Each side presents polarized or contrasting views – the positive and negative biases surrounding the topic.[43] The debate operates according to rules that specify the procedures of the presentation of arguments and counter arguments, with each team presenting a summary statement. Debates may be conducted in f2f or online venues. In the former, there are from three to seven participants directly involved in the activity, with the remainder of the class participating indirectly in the role of judges/evaluators or observers. Because debates are usually organized to be publicly conducted, they are more structured than other f2f small-group activities.

Strengths and limitations. The debate method provides increased opportunity for debaters to develop their extemporaneous listening, reasoning, analytical, and speaking skills. Participants not only have to demonstrate improved alertness and intellectual prowess to discern flaws in their opponents' arguments, but they must increasingly sharpen their skills of bolstering and defending their own team's position by presenting sound evidence and using keen logic. Good debaters are also able to confront differing viewpoints without attacking the person(s) holding such positions.

Limitations of the debate approach are similar to those of the other small group approaches, but one disadvantage that is unique is that in the real world an issue is seldom purely dichotomous. Truth is rarely as simplistic as the black/white debate process makes it out to be. Consequently, experienced instructors advise participants of the limitations, while at the same time, encouraging them to capitalize on the cognitive advantages that accrue by simply experiencing the process of a debate process.

What are the differences for instructors between online and f2f debating?

Another potential limitation is the danger of being so cognitively and emotionally attached to a single polarized viewpoint that individuals may become close-minded to alternative points. Thus, skilled teachers emphasize during the debriefing period after the debate that a key purpose of the process is to promote reflection and modification of opinion among participants and observers alike.

With respect to conducting an online debate[44] instructors recognize that the above principles are applicable but the format is different. For instance, the online version generally relies on video-conferencing software and team members may not be in the same location. The ability to interject or debate may be less spontaneous but when moderated properly can be as effective as being in an f2f environment.

Drama, Role-Plays, and Simulations[45]

Drama. A third category of student-centered techniques is a drama activity. Proponents of the use of drama in teaching assert that it can be utilized in at least some form with any subject in all disciplines.[46] One form may simply be the incorporation of relevant humour, such as projecting an amusing cartoon, comical video clip, music sound-bite, or humourous anecdote as the motivational set of a class period. Incorporating drama in the teaching/learning setting accentuates the affective domain of human life (i.e., the emotional aspect that touches participants' feelings and sentiments).

Some educators believe that "theatre" means to watch or view an event, while "drama" means to live through an event in which people experience the humanizing process of "being in someone else's shoes."[47] The latter can be incorporated into any subject.

Because effective learning is multisensory in nature, effective teachers constantly seek to incorporate a variety of measures that will accelerate, deepen, and stimulate the quality of student learning. Dramatics help achieve this goal. "Motivation" is, in fact, a derivative of the same Latin root for "emotion," which means "to move." Thus, effective teachers add motivational components to their instruction that will cause learners to feel what it may be like to do or think via others' experiences. An advantage of having internet access is that it offers thousands of sources from which instructors can select appropriate drama examples to enhance learning events in their courses.[48] A disadvantage is the sheer number of sites and time needed to search for the material.

Role play. We have found from our own college teaching experience that having students prepare and present f2f or video presentations, which may include short skits, role-plays, or mini-plays, has proved to be a powerful motivator. For instance, in one teacher-education course on Multi-graded Teaching, groups prepared a video on the topic of how to convince parents of the benefits of multi-graded classrooms. In the role play, the principal of a school was conducting a three-way meeting with a family, the multi-grade teacher, and the principal. The goal of the two educators was to try to persuade the reluctant parents to enroll their children in multi-graded classes for the upcoming school year. The actors were so effective in their respective roles that even years later when we met the former class members, they still recounted the hilarity humour of that video, while still remembering its key message. What we all found impressive about that recorded event was that the participants not only had a sound grasp of the relevant research on the topic, but they immersed themselves into the roles with emotion and spontaneity to present a memorable experience.

Another example of how we integrated technology and drama in our own instruction was a simple assignment in an undergraduate course for prospective teachers called *Teaching and Media*. We distributed a video camera to each group of four with directions that they had a two-hour time limit to prepare a two-minute video "commercial" advertising a new university course that they were to develop. The video role-play was to convince viewers to enroll. As with the former example, these video productions were creative, appealing, and humorous and again, these experiences left such an impact on producers and viewers alike that former students still recall the retell experience with pleasure.

The purposes of role plays are to: have students experience the emotions and feelings that arise in a situation; have them gain a fuller understanding of the cognitive processes required in a situation; explore new fields; help them prepare for potentially emotional incidents that they may meet later in their careers; and provide them with increased confidence when they encounter a similar incident in the future.

Strengths of the role play approach are that: (a) students become actively involved in a realistic situation; (b) it can break down cultural or social barriers by having individuals vicariously experience other peoples' feelings; (c) it can compress time in order to present key events and concepts; (d) it can be used to examine a problem situation in virtually any subject; (e) it can involve several people, in both the acting and in the discussion it generates; and (f) it permits participants to rehearse their behaviour in a safe setting that provides a degree of reality, and yet permits some new ideas to be tried without fear of making errors.

Limitations of the role play strategy are: a reluctance, discomfort, or embarrassment that some individuals may experience; it can be time-consuming; and it requires participants to have some background information to help them improvise how the character they are playing would typically behave in the scenario.

Simulations.⁴⁹ A simulation is similar to a role play, but it is typically longer and more complex. One of its purposes is to prepare participants for a future "actual" situation in their work or career. It represents a real-world situation as closely as possible, and it helps people experience the consequences of their actions. Being an artificial situation with authentic characteristics removes the possibility of serious risk that could be present with an actual incident.

TIP
Simulations are more complex than role-plays.

Strengths of the simulation approach are that it: (a) motivates participants and observers; (b) enhances cognitive and skill development in problem-solving and decision-making situations; (c) reduces complicated processes into manageable portions that can be practiced; (d) can be used to assess participants' application of knowledge and performance; (e) sensitizes individuals to the values and experiences of others; and (f) provides "self-feedback" which helps people reflect and improve.

Limitations of simulations are that they are more time-consuming and complicated than role-plays; their effectiveness depends on how real they can be made; players and observers must have a relatively good grasp of the subject at hand, to gain maximum benefit from the activity; and they require participants to invest considerable effort: "they are not a soft option...they take more time than preparing a lecture."⁵⁰

The following guidelines need to be followed:
1. Simulation activities function most effectively in courses that study where crisis decisions must be made, or where best solutions on issues must be selected.
2. Participants must know the procedures to be followed: how to identify and analyze the issues involved; how to formulate, pose, and answer questions about these areas; how to find and weigh evidence; how to ensure equitability, justice, and ethical conduct; and how to mount a strong defense of decisions.
3. The debriefing session must be carefully conducted, permitting participants to explain how they arrived at their decisions, and encouraging others to inquire and probe regarding some of the details of their thinking.

A clear format must be followed.

Examples of simulation experiences that proficient instructors have incorporated into their f2f and online courses are: in Business Administration simulating a corporation's board of directors' meeting where a range of interests are competing; in University Administration simulating a faculty council deciding on who to hire for dean; in Human Relations simulating a student council meeting deciding how to make policy concerning individuals on campus with disabilities; in Chemistry simulating an undergraduate class acting out how various elements move in chemical reactions and how they combine into compounds; in Public Education simulating a school board meeting to formulate policy on the use of prayer and Bible readings in schools; or in Psychology, simulating a group therapy session for troubled adolescents.

Research[51] has indicated that transfer of learning occurs among students when their teachers have effectively combined several of these student-centered strategies. The effect is bolstered when the strategy is accompanied by making provision for the participants to receive specific feedback regarding their performance. Furthermore, the effect of any one of these activities on transfer of learning was less than was the synergistic result of combining several of them.

Other Student-Centered Strategies

A fourth grouping of student-focused experiences consists of projects, discovery and inquiry activities, and problem-solving sessions.[52] The purposes of implementing these group activities are: to enhance students' motivation to increase their knowledge and/or skills in the subject; to cater to the range of learning styles and development levels that are inevitably present in any group of learners; and to help instructors avoid becoming stagnant in their own professional teaching practice. Many of those activities can be assigned individually or collaboratively, and effective instructors intersperse these learning activities throughout the term's work.

Projects. In f2f and online settings projects may take the form of short tasks, papers, reports, readings, case studies, or presentations. A goal of such projects is to permit learners to delve into an area of interest in the content more intensively.

Strengths of such projects are that: students can study a specific area more thoroughly; they can experience a change-of-pace from the regular course routines; and they can experience both the discomfort and the subsequent satisfaction of publicly presenting some of their work.

Limitations of the project method are that: it may consume an inordinate amount of time and effort, and the provision of feedback may not be appropriately timed for maximum student benefit. Effective instructors who assign projects ensure that: (a) the project has clear instructions, that it is task-oriented, and that the task is straight forward; (b) they provide a time limit and clear criteria and expectations by which it will be evaluated; and (c) they make themselves available to answer questions, to clarify points, and to provide periodic formative (i.e., ongoing) assessment of students' progress.

Discovery, inquiry, and problem solving. Effective instructors design independent or small group projects, or shorter assignments, that take the form of discovery or inquiry activities or problem-solving sessions. These types of activities present an interesting problem that students are requested to resolve, by specifically defining the problem, designing procedures for developing solutions, searching for data, analyzing the data and creating probable solutions, verifying these solutions, and reaching plausible conclusions or generalizations.

Instructors must ensure that they mix the levels of questions in the inquiry exercise so as to require students to articulate their understanding of processes, to immediately apply their newly acquired knowledge, to analyze carefully, and to synthesize and assess their reasoning. Further, they ensure that students know that the problem-solving or inquiry activity is connected to the course goals but also that they know the purpose of the investigation and how it will benefit students.

Strengths: Inquiry activities are motivating for learners; students participate and use complex thinking; they employ a variety of resources; and inquiry often promotes spontaneous and open-ended thinking and the creation of new ideas.

Limitations: For teachers to plan, prepare, monitor, and debrief the activity requires substantial time and effort. Effective teachers incorporate this problem-solving approach selectively, not all of the time. Traditional laboratory investigations generally do not generate genuine curiosity among students – rather, they often become tedious and boring.

SUMMARY

In this chapter we have described several methodologies and technologies that effective instructors incorporate into the teaching/learning process. They integrate student-centered strategies: (a) to make the course more interesting; (b) to increase learner motivation; (c) to bolster students' learning with their feeling of acceptance and support; and (d) to ground their instructional decisions within the foundational principles of motivating instruction and ethical values.

Footnotes

[1] Reeves (2009)

[2] Joyce et al. (2009); Ralph (1998)

[3] Freiberg & Driscoll (2000); Jarvis (2006); Saskatchewan Professional Development Unit (1994)

[4] Eggen & Kauchak (2012); Jarvis (2006); Ralph (1998)

[5] Weaver & Cotrell (1987)

[6] Cashin (1990)

[7] Eggen & Kauchak (2012); Le et al. (2010); McElmurry (2012)

[8] Hyerle (1996); Parr (2013)

[9] Louw (2009)

[10] Ziv (1998)

[11] Fan & Le (2012); Venkatesh et al. (2012); Zink (2012)

[12] Davis & Fill (2007); Evans (1994); Kortecamp & Croninger (1996); Reid (2012)

[13] Kilbane & Milman (2014)

[14] Baron (1987); Paul (1987)

[15] Kolovou (2012); Slavin (2011); Tan (2008)

[16] Lambert et al. (2008); Ralph (1995a); Ralph & Walker (2012); Zhan et al. (2011)

[17] Casey-Doecke (2012); McIntosh & Warren (2013); Reich & Daccord (2008); Tang & Austin (2009)

[18] Amabile (1989); Churchill (2009); Hartshorne et al. (2010); Rubin et al. (2010); Teach Thought (2012)
[19] King (1993); Ledlow (2001)
[20] Lorber et al. (2005)
[21] Bibace et al. (1981); Mate et al. (2010); Ralph & Walker (2011, 2012, 2013)
[22] Bolliger et al. (2010); Gacio Harrolle (2012b); Kilty (2013)
[23] Liu (2010)
[24] Wozniak & Silveira (2004)
[25] Nunn (1996); Weimer (1990)
[26] Davidson & Ambrose (1995); Ellison & Wu (2008)
[27] Dixson (2012a); Nunn (1996)
[28] Bonwell (1996); Le, Q. & Le, M. (2012)
[29] Nunn (1996); Ralph (1998)
[30] Hurd et al. (2011); Kember & McNaught (2007)
[31] Huston (1997)
[32] Morse (1995); Yamane (1997); Yu et al. (2010)
[33] Shultz (2012); Weimer (1990); Vanderveen & Wells (2012)
[34] Jackson (2011); Weber (1997)
[35] Yang & Yuen (2010)
[36] Mosteller (1989)
[37] Elliott et al. (2000); Morse (1995); Orlich et al. (2013); Palmer (2010)
[38] Slavin (2011)
[39] Ashton (2012b); Weimer (1997a)
[40] Burden & Byrd (2012); Eggen & Kauchak (2012); Jarvis (2006); Slavin (2011); Weimer (1996b)
[41] Dixson (2012b); Le, T. et al. (2012)
[42] Jarvis (2006); Orlich et al. (2013); Ralph (1998)
[43] Frederick (1987); Ralph (1998)
[44] Anderson & Dron (2011); Schor Ko & Rossen (2008)
[45] Kelly (1976); Slavin (2011); Ralph (1997b)
[46] Gappa-Levi (1996)
[47] Boggs et al. (2007); Kelly (1976); Ralph (1982, 1989, 1997b, 1998)

[48] Banks (2012b)
[49] Christian & Belloni (2012); Frederick (1987); Jarvis (2006); Ralph (1998)
[50] Brookfield (2006); Scott & Schwartz (2012)
[51] Eggen & Kauchak (2012); Garrison & Kanuka (2004); Ma & Harmon (2009)
[52] Chrosniak et al. (2013); Gates (2009); Iiyohi (2013); McGettigan (2013)

CHAPTER 5

PRACTICAL TECHNOLOGY APPLICATIONS TO ENHANCE MOTIVATION

KEY IDEAS

In this concluding chapter we synthesize key points made throughout the book with respect to using technology in teaching, and we present several implementation options that we believe will positively impact the motivation of students.

In this chapter you will learn:
- Introduce a system for integrating technology into your teaching.
- Break down the possibilities to give you a blueprint for easing you into the world of teaching and technology.
- Give you a process for reflecting on your teaching to determine where you are and where your students may be in relation to technology.

- Identify specific technologies that will assist you in making your courses more engaging and effective.
- Provide you with a number of reflective questions to have you think deeply about your situation.

Figure 5.0. Technologies do not automatically improve learning. Instructors must carefully orchestrate the integration of technologies with appropriate methods and strategies at key junctures to maximize learner motivation.

Overview

We have asserted that supporting your teaching with technology can create an improved learning experience for you and your students. We have shown that the basis of good teaching includes a variety of research-backed elements that enhance learning motivation, with technology being a key component. A well-planned and well-executed application of technologies will contribute positively to your pedagogical success and to your students' progress.

With an ever-increasing number of options, the integration of technology in your courses can occur in many forms.[1] To begin this integration, you should answer an initial question: "How could I use technology in this course?" Often instructors do not address whether technology is necessary in a specific situation. They may commit themselves without considering where technology could and could not positively impact the teaching/learning process in a particular context. Thus, a period of review should be central in these early stages. Rushing headlong into a technology application without a clear plan is unwise.[2]

Logical follow-up questions also arise: "Will technology enhance this situation? Are you only concerned that you would not be perceived as current or trendy in your teaching? Has your course content become stale and/or dated?" Answers to these questions may indicate that the content as well as technology needs adjustment. Conducting an audit of your existing style of teaching and the currency of your subject matter will provide a baseline against which to ascertain the appropriate technology to use.[3]

There are several ways to determine the integration of technology. For example, you could survey your colleagues to find what they are doing. Look for actual cases (both positive and negative) in other disciplines. If you decided to focus on observing the actual instructional process, you could learn from any teacher regardless of the subject area. Learning from the successes and failures of others can help you design your technology-implementation plan. Much like requesting a peer-teaching review, you could arrange for a technology audit, by inviting a knowledgeable colleague to assess what you are doing, whether the observe you in action in a face-to-face classroom setting, or how you conduct an online course, or by examining your course syllabus and assignments.[4] Such an audit could help identify integration opportunities. It may be the case that you are only in need of a few suggestions or resources, or conversely your colleague may suggest that a major modification is warranted.

You could also continue to expand your knowledge-base by reviewing some of the literature related to integrating technology in teaching. For instance, a Google search that we made at the time of writing this chapter on the topic of "integrating technology in college and university teaching" yielded nearly 6 million results. Numerous online sites, programs, books, articles, conferences, workshops, and institutional sources are available to provide you with support and increase your understanding in the field. Most universities and colleges have supports available for users of technology, and you should take advantage of their resources. Teaching can be a lonely experience; and some new instructors may think that reaching out and connecting is admitting failure or lacking competence as a teacher.[5] On the contrary, we believe that seeking assistance is actually a sign of your willingness to enhance your teaching practice. It would be worthwhile to make an appointment with your institution's teaching-development center or specialist. You will no doubt find plenty of online or face-to-face support, as well as specific training sessions related to your institution's initiatives. Many schools also offer support through mentorship courses or modules on using technology in teaching or through brief skill-building workshops.[6] Enrolling in such programs will put you in touch with knowledgeable mentors and will connect you with fellow instructors who have similar goals as you. Regular attendance at these events also helps to build professional communities.

What is Your Motivation?

Before making any changes to your instructional practice, you should examine all aspects of your course(s): material, content, assessment, and methods. Don't expect to change all of these components at once. When you have decided that is appears feasible to integrate a specific technology layer, you should reflect on your motivation for doing so, by answering the following questions:

- What outside factors are influencing me to integrate technology?
- Are there colleagues in my department/college/institution who are using it?
- Where did I learn of this change: a presentation I attended, an article I read, or an idea shared by a colleague?
- Did I identify a gap or need from my student course-evaluations?
- What is my level of investment for this change?

Also when considering to incorporate technology, you need to prepare for the re-learning aspects of implementing the change that you may have taken for granted or thought you knew. In fact, you may rediscover aspects of practice that you once held near and dear, but have not recently utilized or may now have no present need for. You will thus also need to ask: "How far am I prepared to go?

Am I ready to leave my comfort zone and perhaps appear less organized in front of students?" As with learning anything new in life, the more experience you gain using it, the more accomplished you will become. Employing a new technology will require a sustained effort to overcome the inevitable setbacks that will emerge. Even these unsuccessful efforts will contribute to your overall knowledge about teaching and they will help you develop a better understanding of what portions to emphasize, adjust, or avoid.[7]

Perhaps you may have you tried incorporating technology component in the past, but you may have had a negative experience that prevented you from pursuing this route. In any case, we are hopeful that you will gain useful information from this manual and combine it with your understanding of creating motivational teaching and learning events. Much of the advice we share throughout the book reflect what we and others have learned through successful and unsuccessful experiences.

What Technology Will Not Do for You

If you are anticipating an amazing or instant transformation because of implementing technology, then you will need to adjust your expectations. Technology, per se, will not improve poor teaching. If you are struggling in your teaching then adding a layer of technology may negatively impact what you are doing in your courses. If you think that trying a "Wizard of Oz" approach will work by hiding behind the technology, you should remember that the curtain will eventually be pulled back exposing the weakness. If you plan carefully, reinforce your relevant skills, and act with relative confidence then you should not be overly concerned.[8]

Furthermore, incorporating technology will not change the quality of your content. There are always times in every course when you will need to share material that is less than exhilarating but that is critical for students' subsequent conceptual understanding in the subject. Certain aspects of your area of study may seem tedious students to master, but their comprehension and application of it is necessary. They may not have yet reached the level of understanding to accept why acquiring certain knowledge is important.

In fact, if you add a layer of technology to the material, students may still struggle with it or may even experience a magnification of misunderstanding. Dressing up the subject matter using technology might make it more palatable, but may diminish their level of learning or distract them from key points. Consider using it only if it will enhance their understanding.

Considerations before Getting Started

When you are new to teaching there is already plenty for you to think about. You may have been hired for your research skills, for your understanding of a certain area of content or discipline, or for your interest in teaching. To implement a full-fledged technology-based teaching program may be very difficult to do at this stage of your career.[9] When you embark on this quest, we would encourage you to start slowly and to focus on meeting the expectations of your students, and in doing so, to choose parts of your content that will remain relatively stable. Attending to stable content means that you will not recreate your technology efforts from scratch, but rather that you will reuse, revise or refine them. Looking for economies of scale in all aspects of preparing for teaching is an important skill for you to master early in your career. For example, you may use similar content in undergraduate and graduate courses, or you may have multiple sections of the same course(s). In these instances you will be able to see more return on your energy investments and time savings.

As part of your institution's goals for enhancing teaching and learning, the use of technology may be viewed as part of your role as a teacher-scholar.[10] Teacher-scholars are expected to work towards excellence in teaching and research, and one aspect of this expectation would no doubt include the integration of technology. The institution and its supporters may have contributed significant resources to upgrade teaching facilities, and as a new faculty member you would be expected to use them appropriately. If a comprehensive institution-wide program is in place, there will be tangible supports available for you.[11] Make sure to take advantage of such support and funding opportunities. If these support programs do not yet exist in your situation, then you may have to work toward initiating them and/or encourage your administration to develop an effective new teacher support program for faculty and students. Rightly or wrongly, if you are younger, your age may influence others to believe that you are more technology savvy or more skilled than are senior faculty.[12]

Another influential trend is that technology is present everywhere in our lives, it is part of our homes and families, and it surrounds us in the media. This omnipresence does not mean that the entire world is completely comfortable with technology, but it is present almost universally. Thus, you must be prepared to deal with expectations regarding the use of technology both from direct and indirect sources. You will encounter a range of students from those whose lives are consumed by technology to others who are terrified or possess little or no interest in embracing it.

An additional piece of advice is that you should not apply technology for the sole purpose of fitting in with your colleagues. They can be great mentors and role models because they have experience in what works, but blindly complying may not be efficient and may result in negative consequences.[13] Putting too much pressure on yourself to adopt the latest device just to appear "with it" may prove unprofitable.

Also, don't feel you have to compete with 'big budget technology productions'. Courses and programs held up as the gold standard had to begin modestly somewhere, which is where you might now be. Often, experts with extensive technology integration may have taken many years to develop their approach, and may have also received significant financial assistance and resource support. As you sensibly develop the integration process in manageable segments, you will gradually find a fit that reflects who you are as an instructor and how you prefer to share your content knowledge.

Another factor to consider is the type of course(s) you are teaching. Our experience suggests that certain content areas such as the natural sciences, history, and kinesiology seem to be more easily enhanced by using technology. Another consideration of using technology for motivation is the format of classes you are teaching. Is your course face-to-face, distance delivery, or mixed mode?[14] Depending on the context you will find some technologies to be more effective for certain situations. In our view, there is really no content that is a perfect fit for support with technology, and there is no content that cannot benefit from support with technology. Courses that do not meet as frequently can benefit by using online technology to build and maintain course community. Having students create websites and blogs for sharing insights and ideas can often bring them closer together, because in such cases there will obviously be more time for reviewing content and connecting with classmates outside of scheduled course time.

Although easier in some cases, technology can positively contribute to *all* subject areas.[15] There may already be an existing selection of technology resources or established routine in your course. What type of content are you working with? Is it primarily theoretical, hands on /practical, or a blend?[16] Remember that you are able to work with technologies classified as *hard* (i.e., the pieces of hardware such as computers, cameras, smartphones, or diagnostic equipment) or *soft* (i.e., the existing strategies and resources available). Are you working with an established program or is it new? If you teach in 'older' programs, technology may be a way of breathing excitement into material that others consider predictable or boring. New programs on the other hand are often ripe for experimentation and innovation, because there are no previous political or territorial issues to restrict you from implementing novel strategies or resources.

Moving Forward

When you have decided to introduce a technology, be sure to plan for its incremental implementation. We think that course design should be iterative, and that good teachers should always be looking to improve.[17] A guideline we like is the *three-year rule*, where one begins with a modest plan in the first year.[18] In the second year you would address any issues that were ineffective the first year and add limited amounts of new content and/or technology. During and at the end of the second year, you would again review and modify what did not work and retain what was working for the third year. Following this plan, you would typically have observed evidence of success with the implementation.

Most courses take three years to evolve into a fully effective learning experience.

Another point to realize is that more preparation time is needed when you are introducing technology. You will first need to familiarize yourself with the tools/resources. Searching out organizations that publish research or that host conferences regarding the technology you are introducing is a beneficial first step.[19] Once you have observed the increased effectiveness, you will want to re-format or re-purpose the course information to fit these choices you made. This entire process will require you to be methodical and reflective. This need to be organized may appear daunting at first, but it will make you more efficient and improve the overall teaching/learning experience for you and the students.

Updating is another important aspect to consider when integrating any technology. Updating will occur in two aspects, the first of which relates to the reality that technologies, themselves, are in constant flux. You will need to update and practice your own technical skills, so that you can be competent in applying the technology and can provide support and guidance for your students as they learn. The second area is that continual updates to software and hardware are simply part of the nature of technology. It is important for you to ensure that any changes to the technology will not detract from your intended purpose for implementing it. If you choose to make an update to a technology, which proves too ambitious, you may find that the update process requires more time than it is worth.

A key factor in all these caveats is that the use of technology means you will need to be prepared well in advance.[20] Our experience has shown that the level of preparation will be greater than even your best efforts in non-technology supported courses. It may also mean that you would be forced to make modifications in short order when required. Realize that websites, electronic files, and other new resources may become quickly available, and may have to be added and reworked to correct errors and enhance the quality of learning. In time past, once a textbook was printed, any errors or updates took considerable time to process. However, today, technology allows you to remain current, but such currency requires you to be well organized and flexible to take advantage of the opportunities to keep up. Your enhanced state of preparation will mean that students will quickly learn what to expect from you, and this factor can contribute positively to their learning success and your credibility as an instructor.

Moreover, your use of *advanced organizers* may support smoother access to what is happening in your course.[21] Advanced organizers are generally text-based content outlines made available to students in advance of the class meeting(s), and which provide a general overview of upcoming course content. These notes do not have to be detailed and in fact, students often appreciate less detail in them. The use of advanced organizers provides you with more flexibility to use your course time to discuss content and explore ideas, instead of focusing on keeping students on the task at hand or on managing their learning. You may feel an occasional need to revert to your previous methods as "a safety blanket," which is natural. However, as you become more comfortable with what you are doing, you will be less inclined to rely on these tried and true ways.

Impact of Technology on You

Another important consideration is that a previous instructional strategy that you have been using may already be effective. This fact will influence the level of technological implementation or change that you wish to make. Furthermore, it can be helpful to complete a learning assessment to reveal information about your own teaching style, rather than the technologies you apply.[22] What type of learner and/or teacher are you? Learning style inventories such as the Kolb or Grasha-Reichmann[23] surveys will provide you with a personal profile of your preferred learning/teaching styles.[24] Check the following site for more details about examining your personal teaching characteristics [http://teaching.uchicago.edu/oldsite/pod/95-96/TeachingWithStyle.htm]. Examining the data produced will help you become more aware of what you bring to your teaching and how you may better stimulate your students' learning. It will also be helpful to have the students complete an inventory such as Kolb's to identify the type of learner they are and how it fits with your approach.[25]

Another concern that new instructors may have is that an overreliance on technology might cause them to lose some spontaneity in their communication with students.[26] We thus advise new faculty members to plan to include times of face-to-face discussions with the regular reading assignments and lecture portions. We suggest that you plan for these unscripted parts of your lessons to promote elements of student belonging, meaningful contribution, and member control as motivators in your courses.

You may also wonder if technology might magnify your faults. Mistakes that you make many seem greater and the impact of technology may cause even more confusion among students. Errors and even disaster occasionally happen at first, but if you are open and willing to admit that you are learning with the students, then they in turn will be more willing to follow your lead, respecting you for working outside of your comfort zone. Some new instructors may feel the use of technology creates a barrier between instructor and students.[27] Therefore, choosing your technology carefully and developing your skills to manage it will mitigate, but not necessarily remove, this barrier. Often what is desired with technology is transparency not invisibility. The advantage of any teaching tool, however basic, should be obvious to the learners. To expect otherwise is not realistic.

Finally, when you decide to begin on a small scale, remember to attempt to progress at a rate with which you feel *slightly* uncomfortable. If you are working in a face to face milieu, you have some control over what is happening. You may have to set-up facilities or adjust a few pieces of equipment, but you have the advantage of looking your students in the eye. Often what you will be doing initially in these situations is showing *Power Point* or *Prezi* presentations, sharing online video and audio clips, and using media projectors and microphones to create connections for students.[28]

It can be fairly straightforward for you to access and use resources. In general, students of all ages typically expect more *edutainment* in the form of some type of technology-based motivational set to get and hold their attention. Not at the expense of compromising your content, but by invoking the motivational principles highlighted in the foregoing chapters, we believe that if you engage your students early, they will be more receptive to the learning journey on which you will embark together. We encourage you to seek ways to use common devices. Especially, look for ways to integrate Web-based apps that will work on smart phones. Most students in your classes will have access to the web and mobility will be an important factor for you to access. They will of course be comfortable with devices they already own; plus, your integration of the phones into your teaching, even in a small way, may expand the possibilities for those students who are underusing their devices. [For example, see http://www.facultyfocus.com/articles/effective-classroom-management/cell-phones-in-the-classroom-whats-your-policy/]

Distance education or distributed education can be a very different experience for you. You will not have as much or in some cases no face-to-face contact with students. As a result you will need to arrange for more obvious supports for them. Redundancy is important for answering student questions, troubleshooting technology, or handling administrative issues.[29] When you cannot have face-to-face interactions, problems can be magnified. Recognizing misunderstandings or paying quick attention to problems does not occur as easily or rapidly online. Another influencing factor is the student expectation of 24/7 service. Today's students are often working on their courses in evenings and weekends, and they will expect you to support them during these times as well. Technology provides the ability for instructors to be connected and available at all times; however, you should clearly lay out what your personal approach will be regarding your availability. Some instructors have virtual offices hours and will turn off their technology outside of these times. Others are willing to be available whenever there is an issue for a student. Decide on your format and follow it.

Technology Tools

Technology and instructional resources will list specific applications or proprietary content. We have tried to steer clear of this approach, because outside of a few tried and true resources, technologies, their resources, sources, and locations are constantly changing. For instance, we have found that if we were to recommend a particular product, it would mean creating a detailed training-session or a "how to" guide for a product that may or may not exist in a year. Instead, throughout this handbook we have presented general references to technologies that will support and enhance your teaching and motivate your students. We have not included all of them. If you want to learn more regarding excellent resources to support your "deep dives" on a tool or technology, then we encourage you to simply "Google an idea" or ask your students and colleagues to share what they have found effective.[30]

We also maintain that being too prescriptive can sometimes

harm the learning process. For you and your students, creative uses of software stimulate the thinking process and transfer control back to the learner.[31] We believe that investing time and energy into a single-use tool is not recommended for you or your students. We refer to the term 'garlic press' meaning a tool that only has one purpose or application. Beware of these garlic presses and also look for new ways to employ a tool that has been designed for limited use. Some technologies, especially emerging social media applications, have multiple uses, some of which may be negative.[32] If the possibility exists that using a technology will adversely impact students in any way, then we urge you not to use or recommend it. This warning includes any type of bullying, stalking, or violating privacy. We later discuss establishing a safe and productive online environment.

An important aspect for anyone utilizing technology is to first locate, learn, and evaluate the tools or software you are considering.[33] Make use of the questions shown on these pages to guide your evaluation of a tool or item of software.

Critical Questions

There are a number of practical questions one must ask when evaluating any type of technology:
- What cost is associated with this tool or software?
- What equipment is needed for the facilitator and for participants?
- What is its ease of use? Is special training required?
- What kinds of support systems are available for this tool? Where do users get help?
- What happens when the technology doesn't work? Can you still communicate without it? What kind of backup plan is needed?

What you know about your technology is crucial to the way it is implemented.

Practicalities aside, it is also important to consider the effect a new technology will have on what you do. Communication theorist Marshall McLuhan and his son Eric identified four laws of media that described the effects that technology has on society.[34] These laws provide a useful framework for evaluating the role technology plays in the way we communicate and teach. You may find this framework to be a useful lens through which you can put technology into focus for your own instructional setting. It may be more helpful for those already using technology, but we think all instructors should find it applicable.

Enhance

- What human trait or experience does the new medium enhance?
- What is the intended function of the new medium or technology?
- What does it improve or make more efficient?
- Does it extend part of the human body or one or more of the senses?
- Does it extend some aspect of the human mind (e.g., memory)?
- Does it extend the individual, the group, or society?

Obsolesce

- What pre-existing technology, method, system, or medium does the new medium make obsolete?
- What older technology does the new medium replace?
- What does it render unnecessary?
- What procedures does it bypass?
- What happens to the old medium that is rendered "obsolescent:" does it disappear entirely, become an art object, or find a new niche?

Retrieve

- What technology, method, system, or medium that was previously obsolesced or abandoned does the new medium retrieve?
- What archaic elements are made relevant again? (e.g., tone of voice, facial expression)

Reverse
- When fully utilized or pushed to its extreme, what will the new medium or technology reverse into?
- What effects will the new medium create that are opposite to what was originally intended? (Are there ways that a new communication tool blocks or hinders communication?)
- What contradictions are inherent in the new technology?

Levels of Technology Integration

There are many options for integrating technology in your teaching. We present them in a manner that will allow you to examine your situation and determine what you are able to offer students. If you are new to using technology in your teaching the first level is a sensible place to start.

Level One: Basic Technologies
(Students will likely expect more.)
- Online notes/handouts/PDFs.
- Online resources, textbook, web links
- E-mail
- Online drop box
- Electronic presentations

At *Level One* you are presenting your content in a more accessible format and are encouraging communication. If your existing course material such as handouts, lecture notes, and presentation files are already in a digital format, then you will be able to post them to a course website for students to easily access. Most word processing and presentation software will allow you to export your files in a PDF format making them easy to read on any computer or platform. PDF is the lowest common denominator for sharing that creates an image of your files, making them universally readable and printable. Many textbook publishers are providing online content to support the books they are selling to your students. Linking or signing up for access to these resources is easily done, and can provide you and your students will high quality support for your courses.

Although considered an older form of technology, email is still a key way to maintain contact with your students.[35] A mailing list of institutional addresses for students is often provided to instructors and students can link their University or College address to other accounts that they check regularly. Online drop boxes help to prevent lost material and create an easy method to share resources with students. They are easy to manage and allow you to create private areas for specific files and groups of students. Most people have worked with *Power Point, Prezi, Keynote,* or other presentation software. Applications that allow you to legibly and easily create slides can be an effective way of organizing and sharing information. Take advantage of using images, videos, and graphics to enhance the messages you present. Text heavy presentations with little or no engaging visuals will be de-motivating compared to content that visually stimulates learners and clearly demonstrates complex concepts.

Level Two: More Interaction

- Learning management systems
- Discussion forums/boards
- Podcasts
- Video
- Blogs
- Social media (e.g., *Twitter, Facebook*)

Level Two requires more diversity and more investment of time/energy by the instructor. You are beginning to go beyond basic course support to include enriching content. You may begin to discover the power of online learning based on successes through Level One. You may be thinking of moving all of your material online and making it available through a learning management system.[36] This process will give your students even better access to the material and to each other. Posting questions in a course discussion forum is a first step in diversifying your evaluation. It requires students to become familiar with the content, share their thoughts about it publicly, and comment on the postings of others. Group discussions can be moderated by students in your course to further deepen their connections with the material. You may continue to include information from other sources in the form of audio or video podcasts. Noted educators, commentators, or organizations may provide regularly offered resources such as podcasts to supplement your course content.

You are able to take advantage of the knowledge and efforts of others to promote your students' engagement and motivation. Remember that linking to a public online file is not a violation of copyright and is a good way to save you from reinventing something that is already available. For content that is not available, you may begin to create your own. There is a good chance that you already have the tools you need to create useful content for your courses. It is easy to use your phone or computer to record a narrative of a process or a portion of content. However, ensure that the length of these talks is as short as possible. Often having a loose script prepared in advance will help you cover key points and not become sidetracked or long-winded. You also may have taken a short course on video creation or begun to experiment with your camera. Through these skills you may begin to add your own video resources to your course. These items may be lectures directed to the camera with images or graphics included to allow students to review concepts before and after you address them in class. Don't worry about creating Hollywood quality material at this stage, because seeking perfection can be too time-consuming and impractical. As long as the main idea is clear and the visual is in focus, you can often use the resources you already have or can capture. A lower quality video production with occasional mistakes is sometimes more memorable for students.

Level Three: Asynchronous Online Course Delivery

- Animation
- Creative forms of evaluation and assignment completion
- Student generated content
- Student led assignments

At *Level Three* you would be usually involved in online-only courses and have some form of technology or instructional support. Your comfort level with basic technologies would be high and you would be concentrating your efforts on maximizing the learning experience for your students. You would be seeking to make complex concepts more concrete. This goal may mean creating visual representations of processes or interrelated activities. In the sciences, for example, it may mean creating a 3D model of a body system or a chemical phenomenon at an atomic level. These resources are time-consuming creations, but they can be uniquely helpful and are often not readily available from other sources.

You may also begin to support your students' use of technology to create material that you will assess toward their course grade. You or other instructors may provide hands-on workshops for students to help them to expand their technological skills beyond the basic level. This process might mean showing them how to create a blog, to reflect and share their thoughts, or to use a wiki to collaborate virtually as a group.[37] Often the added layer of technology acts as a motivator and a break from what they may have experienced in their other courses. You will continue to hand over more control to students, knowing that they are becoming increasingly competent and confident with applying the technology.

Again you notice that in this list we have not provided names of specific tools, but have instead referred to what the tools can do. The changing nature of technology means that there is always a newer or different tool, app, or software. For us to suggest a specific tool will not allow you to find a technology that fits your teaching style and instructional needs. We thus encourage you to be alert for individuals and groups who are exploring new products. Be attuned to what your students are already using and be open to acknowledge and incorporate their existing knowledge and skill sets into the course. Also allow for different tools to do the same job. Being too prescriptive can hinder your success and that of your students. We believe you should only apply limits when what is happening is negatively impacting student progress.

What about the Students?

One of the elements of instructional technology that can often be overlooked is the skill that students bring to your courses.[38] There is a belief among many educators that all students are multi skilled in the use of technology and are well able to adapt. However, we have observed that often in university this scenario is not the case.[39] There are certain skill sets that they do or do not possess. Most universities provide short courses on basic technologies for students and faculties. These support offices may also design and deliver training specific to particular courses.⁴⁰ There are many free online services available, as well. If you find a good technology development resource, we encourage you share it freely with your students. Having useful resources will allow the students to take control of their own development and free you from having to play the role of technologist or trainer.⁴¹

You will encounter a range of students from those whose lives are consumed by technology to others who are terrified or possess little or no interest in embracing it.

Key questions you will need to ask on this subject are:
- Do students have the skills specific to your course design and content?
- Do they have access to the needed technology? For instance, more and more institutions are developing learning commons areas.
- Are students motivated to use the technologies? Depending on where they are in terms of technological maturity, they may have or have not developed positive attitudes towards technology.
- Can they be motivated?

Failure to address the needs of the students will derail even the best-planned teaching and learning experiences. Again, it is important as an instructor to know as much about your instructional styles as possible, and to understand where your strengths are and where you need to grow. This self-knowledge is no different for your students. Having them complete a personal-skills profile or learning inventory will also assist them as they proceed in your courses.

Technology and Teaching Using the Internet

A common use of technology in teaching is to take advantage of the opportunities presented by the Internet.⁴² The Internet delivers information, facilitates communication between instructor and students and between students, creates connections with experts, and provides instructors and students with numerous ways to enhance pedagogy, learning, and assessment.

An important aspect of using the Internet is developing an online presence.[43] Instructors' online presence has replaced the physical office location as a first point of contact for students. Your web presence may be represented by a website that presents what you do and who you are. It may contain links to, or copies of, your publications and the organizations to which you belong, and it can thus serve as a helpful contact point for current and perspective students.

You will also want to have a website for the individual courses you teach. Course websites can serve a number of purposes. A course homepage is critical for online-only or distance education courses. Options for creating course homepages include learning to program using an editor such as *Dreamweaver* or using existing sites such as *Google, Blogger* or *Weebly*.[44] You should check with your institution to see if they already utilize a *Learning Management System* (LMS). Similar to a website, a LMS is usually template-based, thereby eliminating any need for you to become a technician. Your institution will typically provide course websites, and will also have dedicated web-server space available for teaching related material.

Online Discussion Boards

One of the most obvious applications of technology to motivate learners takes place in online teaching and learning environments in the form of online discussions. Closely connected to making discussion boards available to your students, is the requirement that you will need to develop the ability to be a facilitator of online discussions.[45] Online facilitation is important to guide your students' understanding, to foster communication, and to engage learners who are not in a face-to-face setting. In face-to-face courses online discussion helps you create depth that is often not possible in regular group situations or classroom lectures. Many learners prefer discussion boards because of being able to engage in the course content to a level that they have not experienced in more traditional situations.[46] Not surprisingly, many of the effective tools of online learning or distance education can easily be integrated into face-to-face courses as well.

A challenge facing instructors with online discussion boards is that instead of being in control of all aspects of the course, you will move from the traditional role of *teacher* to the support role of *facilitator*.⁴⁷ You need to determine the role you will fill in the online discussion. Will you lead introductory community building activities and then gradually fade away as the members take the lead? Will you provide support for solving technical problems and for assisting newcomers? Will you ensure that, as the instructor, you will make a conscious effort to share who you are with students, and to openly demonstrate your personality? Behaving and responding in a way that students can relate to will allow students to reciprocate, and it will positively contribute to the communication climate in the course. You will no doubt find that you will have to use humor sparingly, because online environments, especially those that rely on text, are not well-suited to communicate the precise nature or innuendos of jokes, with which you may have been accustomed to delivering in regular classes. Also do your best to respond to the *entire* group; and avoid engaging in one-on-one conversations that may lead to excluding, isolating, or ignoring learners.⁴⁸

Integrating online discussion can be an effective learning experience when it is well-planned and supported by the instructor. Taking the time to plan for an online session goes a long way to creating a positive learning experience.⁴⁹ This planning process begins by providing members with an agenda well in advance. Ensuring the ongoing success of your online group can also be made easier by creating a set of procedures for all participants to follow. Make sure you review the course rules with participants in advance, especially so that they understand the importance of respecting each other. If you present meaningful and relevant topics in which students to engage, they will be more likely to contribute and to learn. Communicating the plan for the term is crucial for online students. Because you may not have the opportunity to respond to them instantly, they will need to know how to keep organized until you contact them. Students who are not self-motivated will need to learn to use both long- and short-term planners in order to meet important deadlines.

Online discussion boards are typically organized into topics or categories of conversation that contain a number of individual discussions. Messages within threads are built in layers in that participants progressively reply to individual messages by adding comments to those previously made by their peers. The two main types of online discussions are *synchronous* and *asynchronous*, the former taking place when learners and instructor are engaged with each other at the same time.[50] By contrast, asynchronous discussion takes place without requiring participants to be online at the same time. Each form has its own characteristics and courses usually employ both methods. Awarding part of a student's grade for the depth of their online contributions and engagement will motivate learners to go beyond the "I agree" and "Me too" posts. By inviting participants to share their thoughts or to relate the course content to their own life experiences will allow them to post contributions without worrying about having the "right" answer, and it will open up the discussion to a wider variety of ideas. If you only require students to add a specified number of posts, then online discussion may become a pointless exercise that will not promote deep learning. Assigning roles to course members can help online communication go beyond a simple exchange of information to productive communication and authentic learning.[51] Furthermore, the group's dynamics will evolve as participants systematically take on and switch roles as the course progresses. Assigning and exchanging roles in a planned manner can give participants a framework upon which to base their responses and it can help ensure balanced levels of involvement from everyone.

Often students in a course with an online component may want to continue the connections they have made, and they may also want to access the resources that you have shared with them. Check to see if this access can be facilitated through your organization's existing Information Technology infrastructure. Unless your institution specifically supports open online environments, choosing an online learning technology that can continue to live and grow will often be a better choice for the long-term learning of your students and long-term viability of your course community.

Developing a Technology Supported Professional Learning Community

Another key skill is developing a *Professional Learning Community* or PLC, sometimes known as a *Networked Learning Community* or NLC (if facilitated by technology).[52] An NLC takes advantage of the resources students and outside professionals have to share. As your learners move into their chosen professions, the networks and knowledge they developed as students will benefit their ongoing understanding of both the process and the content they experienced, which ma in turn assist them to make valuable connections related to their securing of future employment.

Ensuring the Success of Your Online Learners

There are many levels of attention that need to be addressed to ensure that your learners are successful in your online courses.[53] At the start of each online course it is important for the instructor to lead introductory community-building activities.[54] Investing time during the first meeting(s) or module(s) allows participants to become familiar with group procedures and expectations. You can incorporate socializing activities to create group camaraderie, to create members' comfort level, and to ensure that the technology is working. You should also provide support for technical troubles that inevitably arise, so that individuals unfamiliar with the online environment will know what procedures to follow. Arranging optional meetings before courses begin can help boost the confidence of those new to online learning environments.

You will need to provide access to resources for your participants, such as alerting them if the software provider has any tutorials or help files available. Most LMSs have a homepage and links to support participants new to the software. There may be minimum software requirements or plug-ins to download to run particular applications. Most LMS developers offer instructions and free downloads of these components on their websites.

Providing students with connections to knowledgeable IT contacts in your organization can make the online support process easier to access for those needing it. These skilled support people are excellent at dealing with specific issues that you as an instructor may not have the expertise or time to resolve. Also look for publicly available help and tutorials in places like *YouTube* or *Lynda.com*. Whenever possible, plan ahead and distribute support materials to members before the online course, meeting, or event commences.

Another strategy is to organize a "meet and greet" session. This meeting is a low-stakes event where the primary goal is to ensure that participants can connect to the online environment without difficulty. Often arranging the last few days before a course begins as "open meeting times" will help students to become more confident in using the technology in a safe and supportive environment. They can try different options, and can find a comfort level by practicing locating and/or using resources.

You could implement one method of communicating online, called the WRITE way by incorporating each of its following components:[55]

- (W)armth
- (R)esponsiveness
- (I)nquisitiveness
- (T)entativeness
- (E)mpathy

Also be alert to the inevitability that conflict can arise from:

- Misunderstanding
- Misinterpretation
- Criticizing deeply held beliefs

As well, be cognizant that conflict can be reduced by:
- Modeling desired behaviour
- Rephrasing directions
- Moving some conversations to private venues

Online Assignments and Assessment

Online LMSs can also be used to gather and share assessment materials. Rubrics can be easily posted for students to access. An iterative assignment process takes place that allows you to share documents within groups in the form of a *wiki*, or it allows students to submit drafts, which you can annotate and return for further editing. The *Track Changes* feature in MS Word can be a valuable tool for giving students feedback in the form of inserted comments on their written submissions. An online submission tool such as *Dropbox* can also be used for the submission of student assignments and as a place for groups to find instructions regarding course assignments.

Web-based testing and student assessment. A key principle to follow when evaluating student work is to assess a wide variety of their assignments or work samples.[56] When you are working online two types of evaluation are generally used, the first of which is formative assessment. It can be used to improve student performance during the duration of a course. Keeping in regular contact with your students online is important, because online courses provide little or no face-to-face contact. When you are active online students will realize that you are involved and interested, and it will also demonstrate that you are serious about verifying their understanding of the material.

The second type of assessment is *summative*, which generally takes place at the end of a course and is used to evaluate overall student/participant progress or their final achievement levels in the course. Summative assessment is also important to instructors for influencing their redesign of the course/program. With any online course you can use blogs or online surveys to assess student learning. Surveys are fairly easy to construct, and you can collect and use data from a variety of tools available to conduct anonymous surveys online. One of the popular free online survey applications is *Survey Monkey*.[57] Another good site that provides a host of possible assessment tools and Classroom Assessment Techniques (CATs) for face-to-face classrooms or online courses can be found at https://sites.google.com/site/facilitatinggroupsonline/course-evaluation .

Improving critical thinking via educational technology. Using technology to enhance students' critical thinking can also be an important influence on their motivation. Learners should use the Internet to gain a wider array of viewpoints or a broader perspective on issues. Be sure to have them search the Web to uncover dissenting views on ideas and theories, in order to help them begin to question and/or reflect on issues and alternate positions, rather than blindly accepting them without critique. Having students publicly publish their own positions or opinions, or encouraging them to judge arguments differently will increase their critical and creative thinking abilities. Furthermore, having them post their arguments and rationales and receive feedback from their peers or other readers, worldwide, can be a powerful learning experience.

You Made It Now What?

As with any modification to your teaching, you will need to conduct an evaluation of the process. It is important to keep track of the positive and negative elements that emerged during this period of change and transformation. In addition to course evaluations, you will want to arrange other ways to inform your assessment of the process. Although program evaluation reports are helpful, you can also arrange focus groups with former students to collect feedback. Gathering honest responses designed to inform your professional development will be beneficial to you in improving the teaching/learning process.

Moreover, the evaluation process will make students feel engaged and will stimulate their vested interest in the success of your course(s). It will help you address key questions, such as: What is the future of the course? Is it positioned as a key requirement? Should you make plans to revise the course on a yearly basis? If you have chosen technology that is new, will it need to be updated regularly? For instance, you may recognize that stable technology components will not require constant updating and may be a better choice compared to seeking the next latest technological trend. In our view, stability and reliability should always trump uncertain promises of novel or fashionable functionality.

To us, the fact that you have reached this point in the book shows your commitment to enhancing the overall teaching/learning effectiveness in your coursework. Moreover, you may still be asking yourself, "What can I do at this juncture regarding my current skills?" We suggest that you could continue to:

- Think about your personal mannerisms and non-verbal communication;
- Work on your oration skills;
- Keep up to date in your subject material;
- Consider what students share in your course evaluations;
- Make your instruction relevant to their lives; and
- Build connections to the larger community.

You may become overwhelmed when you focus on developing as a teacher, because technology is only one of several components to be addressed. That being said, we also contend that with some dedicated time on your part, you will be able to integrate some facet of technology in order to enhance your teaching and support the success of your learners.

SUMMARY

Hopefully this chapter has opened your eyes to the possibilities of using technology in your teaching. There are many simple ways to enhance the teaching and learning experience through the application of technology. Rather than using random approach if you design a system for integrating technology into your teaching the experience will be more effective and easier on you. It is key to assess where you are and where your learners may be to achieve the most benefit. Begin with a focused plan that does not include too much innovation. Execute your plan and assess its effectiveness. Change what you can then plan for increasing your integration of technology. Take advantage of the many inventories that can give both you and your students an understanding of your/their learner style. Carefully consider the three stages of technology we present and find a path that resonates with who you are and the goals you have for your learning environment. Evaluate the possibilities to give you a blueprint for easing you into the world of teaching and technology. We have identified general categories of technologies that will assist you in making your courses more engaging and effective. You will need to engage in further exploration to find the specific applications that work best for you. Rather than provide you with a one-shot experience we hope you will revisit this chapter as your courses evolve. Reread the reflective questions to understand where the successes have been and where the challenges remain.

Concluding Thoughts: Inspiring Students

This book has highlighted that students must be engaged in their own learning, and that their motivation invokes both the art and science of teaching. To develop your motivational skills you will need to not only regularly and intentionally reflect on your teaching practice but also on your own experiences as a learner. For instance, you should regularly make time to think about the instructors or coaches who motivated you. What made them stand out? How did they approach connecting you to the tasks in the program? What particular traits and actions inspired you? You no doubt found that good teachers will often give learners the authority to make certain decisions regarding aspects of content, process, and evaluation. You may also find in your teaching that once the participants share ownership in helping direct some of the components, then they will be more willing to embrace in the activities. We hope that you will also seize opportunities to help learners make authentic connections in the wider world and to deepen their learning experience.

If you share your passion for the content and related pedagogy, you may find that your students begin to develop a similar enthusiasm. Again we think that if you are open with students about specific facets of your own professional learning journey, you will find that they will reciprocate. Once the group becomes acquainted and builds mutual trust, then authentic communication/discussion will grow. In turn, your nurturing of this open relationship will not only demonstrate that you enjoy the process, but that students are welcome to participate freely and have fun with the material as well.

One result of creating this positive work climate will permit the group to set high but attainable expectations for students' achievement, which in turn will prompt them to invest more deeply in their own learning. They will be more amenable to consider going beyond what they think they are capable of, and will ultimately undergo a more rewarding learning experience. Accomplishing difficult learning tasks may take extra time, and students will doubtless experience frustration, but they will realize that you are dedicated to supporting them in this quest. In fact, asking more from your students will mean a greater commitment from you. Your job will not always to be "the expert," but to be a mentor, as they learn to be both independently and interdependently successful. You will still need to be prepared to occasionally "step in to a situation," but on the other hand, for you to monopolize the learning environment may lead them to be resentful. That is, they may become angry about not having freedom to explore within the boundaries of the course or activity. They will need to see that you are willing to learn along with them, and that you are open to entertain question and to explore alternatives, yourself.

Another positive motivational premise is to learn from thinkers who have provided insight and inspiration regarding how to enhance the teaching/learning enterprise. Some of these renown writers worth consulting include Ernest Boyer, John Dewey, Paulo Freire, Parker Palmer, Anne Sullivan, and Lee Shulman. These educators have spent considerable time reflecting on their own noteworthy practice and on sharing their ideas regarding learners, learning, and the mentorship role you occupy.

Your motivation and inspiration may lead one or more of your protégés along a path they never thought of pursuing previously. Many people share stories about a specific teacher or coach who engaged them in new fields, which eventually led them into an entirely new career. You, too, can encourage students to go beyond what you may have prepared in a lesson or module; and if students contact you because they are enthused about something in your course, we urge you to encourage them to pursue such interests. It takes courage for them to seek the possibilities. Welcome their enthusiasm and support their explorations.

We hope that you will maintain your enthusiasm and passion for your discipline; and that you will lead by example and let others observe the inspiration of your students. Remind yourself why you chose not only to be a teacher but to teach in a particular area. Think of those satisfying moments when you realized that the work you expended all made sense; and reflect on how you might influence others as they seek similar rewards.

You may have taught the same content many times, but remember your students are new to it, as illustrated by an anecdote regarding baseball legend, Joe DiMaggio. He was asked why he tried so hard each game. His response was that not everyone in the stands had seen him play before, and he wanted to do his best each time he performed so everyone who observed him would witness his devotion and skill. Should we as teachers similarly want to perform our best each time we meet a fresh group of students?

Footnotes

[1] Ball (2011); Felver (2012); Hagner (2000): Madden et al. (2013); Wiles & Bondi (2011)

[2] Ducharme (2012); Skelton (2007); Smith et al. (2007); White & Weight (1999)

[3] Dill (2000); MacPherson (2014); Parker et al. (2011); Tien & Fu (2008)

[4] Kortecamp & Croninger (1996); Lee et al. (2009); Ralph & Noonan (2004); Ralph & Yang (1993)

[5] Dunlap & Lowenthal (2011); Le Maistre & Pare (2010); Ralph (1995b, 1996)

[6] Cho et al. (2011); Coutinho (2010); Hubball et al. (2010); Yorke (2011)

[7] Biggs & Tang (2011); Gibbs & Coffey (2004); Tsai & Chai (2012)

[8] Elzarka (2012); Harris & Hofer (2011); Parkay et al. (2012); Smythe (2012)

[9] Bowe (2011); Gibbs (1995); Lepi (2013a, 2013b); Reid (2012)

[10] Barrett et al. (2012); Kyei-Blankson et al. (2009); Zygouris-Coe et al. (2009)

[11] Bowe (2011); Breidenstein et al. (2012); Kalota & Hung (2013); Lehman & Conceicao (2013); Westerberg (2013)

[12] Prensky (2010); Tweed (2013); Weas (2010)

[13] Feldman et al. (2010); Hall & Lowe (2014); Mukherjee (2012); Organization for (2003); Piscioneri (2012); Wang-Wei-Tsong (2009); Wasserstein et al. (2007)

[14] Coswatte & Ives (2013); Hoffstetter (2012); Laverty et al. (2012); Mouzakis (2008); Spies (2011)

[15] Bennett & Scholes (2001); Gill (2012); Guertin (2012); Guest Writer (2012); Howles (2007); Orlich et al. (2013)

[16] Davis & Fill (2007); Owston (2013); Smith (2005); Smith et al. (2007)

[17] Bergin (2001); Couthino & Bottentuit (2010); Gururajan et al. (2011); Lu et al. (2011)

[18] Bork (2001); Dunn (2013); Hanewald & Ng (2011); Hurn (2012)

[19] Boyle (2013); and see websites of *Society for Teaching and Learning in Higher Education* (STLHE) and *Society for Information Technology and Teacher Education* (SITTE).

[20] Benson & Ward (2013); Duffy & Rimmer (2008); Guhlin (2009)

[21] Aslani et al. (2013); Kaufman (2009)

[22] Bibace et al. (1981); Brandt (1997); Brookfield (1995, 1996); Leung et al. (2003)

[23] Grasha (1996); Grasha & Yangarber-Hicks (2000); Grasha-Riechmann (n.d.); Kolb & Kolb (2005)

[24] Beachem (1996); Smith (2008)

[25] Kolb & Kolb (2005); Solvie & Sungur (2012)

[26] Conley (2012); Dunning (2014); Hoofnagle (2012); Walsh (2013)

[27] Al-Senaidi et al. (2009); Graf & Liu (2009); Oliveira et al. (2011); Tsai & Chai (2012); Tweed (2013); Warschauer (2011)

[28] Foster (2006); Margaryan et al. (2011); Simon (2012)

[29] Bruffee (1994, 1995); Dale (2013); Hagner (2000); Phillips (2003)

[30] Lieberman & Friedrich (2010); Showers et al. (1987); Shulman (1987, 1993); Venkatesh et al. (2012); Yelon (2006)

[31] Auttawutikul et al. (2013); Conrad & Donaldson (2012); Kates (2012); McIntosh & Warren (2013); Reyes (2013b); Wray (2012)

[32] Anastasiades, (2012); Car (2010); Fried (2008); Moreno (2012); Wang (2011)

[33] Feng et al. (2011); Guzzetti et al. (2010); Herold (2010); Kurilovas & Sėrikovienė (2010); Nicholas (2011); Sadasivam et al. (2010); Tsai et al. (2012); Williams et al. (2009)

[34] Chen & Kao (2012); McLuhan & McLuhan (1992)

[35] Uddin & Jacobson (2013)

[36] Al-Ajlan (2012); Laverty et al. (2012); Lonn & Teasley, (2009); Rubin et al (2010); Soto-Rojas (2012); Soto-Rojas & Martinez-Mier (2012)

[37] Cooper (2012); Friberg (2012); Kumar (2012); Morrone (2012)

[38] Feng et al. (2011); Kahan Kennedy & Hinkley (2011); Kyei-Blankson, et al. (2009).

[39] Margaryan et al. (2011); Ogrenci (2012); Tsai et al. (2012); Waycott et al. (2000)

[40] Goering (2012); Kalota & Hung (2013); Nilson (2010)

[41] Bell et al. (2013); New Media (2013); Rivard (2013)

[42] Barrett et al. (2012); Carman (2010); Carnegie (n.d.); Fiedor (2012); Joyner (2012); Lynch & Roecker (2007); O'Hara & Pritchard (2012)

[43] Barbour & Marshall (2012); Hickerson & Giglio (2009)

[44] Chen (2010); Churchill (2009); Feng (2012)

[45] Hunter-Rainey (2012); McCarthy et al. (2010); Oliva & Gordon (2012)

[46] Costa et al. (2014); Hurd et al. (2011); Weller (2012)

[47] Chickering & Ehrmann (1996); Fidishun (n.d.); Waters (2012).

[48] McFerrin & Christensen (2013)

[49] Eichinger & Lombardo (2003); Gavrin (2012a, 2012b); Ng, E. et al. (2011); O'Hara (2012); Wozniak & Silveira (2004)

[50] Cheon & Grant (2009); Dennis et al. (2008); De Wever et al. (2009); Jones (2012); Oztok et al. (2013)

[51] De Wever et al. (2009); Nandi et al. (2012); Weimer (1997b)

[52] Albon & Trinidad (2002); Ashton (2012a); Chi-Yin Yuen & Hao Yang (2010); Cook et al. (2010)

[53] Grajek (2013); Owens (2012); Ralph (2005); Saxena Arora & Raisinghani (2011); Smith (2005).

[54] Albon & Trinidad (2002); Lu et al. (2011); Rolf (2012)

[55] Lewis (2000)

[56] Pappas (2013c); Rolf (2012); Stödberg (2012); Swan et al (2006)

[57] See website http://www.surveymonkey.com

References

Abdallah, S. (2011). Learning with online activities: What do students think about their experience? In E. Ng., N. Karacapilidis, & M. Raisinghani (Eds.), *Dynamic advancements in teaching and learning based technologies: New concepts* (pp. 96-121). Hershey, PA: Information Science Reference.

Acree Walsh, J., & Dankert Sattes, B. (2005). *Quality questioning: Research-based practice to engage every learner.* Thousand Oaks, CA: Corwin/Sage/Appalachia Educational Laboratory.

Adlakha, V., & Aggarwal, A. (2011). Minimal functionalities of course management systems: A faculty perspective. In E. Ng., N. Karacapilidis, & M. Raisinghani (Eds.), *Dynamic advancements in teaching and learning based technologies: New concepts* (pp. 122-141). Hershey, PA: Information Science Reference.

Ahedo, M. (2011). Towards an effective ICT-based university learning: The tacit and the interactive dimensions. In E. Ng., N. Karacapilidis, & M. Raisinghani (Eds.), *Dynamic advancements in teaching and learning based technologies: New concepts* (pp. 316-332). Hershey, PA: Information Science Reference.

Ahluwalia, D., & McCreary, M. (n.d.). *Teaching students with disabilities: A guide for faculty.* Saskatoon, Saskatchewan: University of Saskatchewan.

Al-Ajlan, A. (2012). A comparative study between e-learning features, methodologies, tools and new developments for e-learning. In E. Pontes (Ed.), *Methodologies, tools and new developments for e-learning* (pp. 191-214). Rijeka, Croatia: InTech. Retrieved from

http://www.intechopen.com/books/methodologies-tools-and-new-developments-for-e-learning/a-comparative-study-between-e-learning-features

Albon, R., & Trinidad, S. (2002). Building learning communities through technology. In K. Appleton, C. Macpherson, & D. Orr (Eds.). *Lifelong learning conference: Refereed papers from the 2nd International Lifelong Learning Conference* (pp. 50-56). Yeppoon, Queensland, Australia, 16-19 June. Rockhampton: Central Queensland University Press. Retrieved from http://library-resources.cqu.edu.au:8888/access/detail.php?pid=cqu:1836

Allen, I., & Seaman, J. (2010). *Learning on demand online education in the United States, 2009.* Retrieved from http://sloanconsortium.org/publications/survey/pdf/learningondemand.pdf

Al-Senaidi, S., Lin, L., & Poirot, J. (2009). Barriers to adopting technology for teaching and learning in Oman. *Computers & Education, 53,* 575–

590. Retrieved from http://www.sciencedirect.com/science/article/pii/S0360131509000827

Amabile, T. (1989). *Growing up creative: Nurturing a lifetime of creativity.* New York: Crown.

Amabile, T., & Kramer, S. (2011). *The progress principle: Using small wins to ignite joy, engagement, and creativity at work.* Boston, MA: Harvard Business Review Press.

American Association for Higher Education. (1996*). Principles of good practice for assessing student learning.* Washington, DC: AAHE Assessment Forum.

American Psychological Association (APA). (2010). *Publication manual of the American Psychological Association.* (6th ed.). Washington, DC: Author.

Ames, R., & Ames, C. (1984). Introduction. In R. Ames & C. Ames (Eds.), *Research in motivation in education: Vol. 1. Student motivation* (pp. 1-11). Toronto, ON: Academic.

Amirault, R., & Visser, Y. (2010). *The impact of e-learning programs on the internationalization of the university.* New York: Nova Science Publishers.

An, S., & Lipscomb, R. (2010). Instant mentoring: Sharing wisdom and getting advice online with E-mentoring. *Journal of the American Dietetic Association, 110*(8), 1148-1155. doi:10.1016/j.jada.2010.06.019

Anastasiades, P. S. (Ed.). (2012). *Blended learning environments for adults: Evaluations and frameworks.* Hershey, PA: Information Science Reference, IGI Global.

Anderson, D. (2011). Adult learning with audience response systems. *Academic Exchange Quarterly, 15*(3) on-line. Retrieved from http://rapidintellect.com/AEQweb/cho4918.htm

Anderson, K., Walker, K., & Ralph, E. (2009). Practicum teachers' perceptions of success in relation to self-efficacy (perceived competence). *The Alberta Journal of Educational Research, 55*(2), 157-170. Retrieved from http://ajer.journalhosting.ucalgary.ca/ajer/index.php/ajer/article/viewFile/724/696

Andrews, T., Davidson, B., Hill, A., Sloane, D., & Woodhouse, L. (2011). Using students' own mobile technologies to support clinical competency development in speech pathology. In A. Kitchenham (Ed.), *Models for interdisciplinary mobile learning: Delivering information to students* (pp. 247-264). Hershey, PA: Information Science Reference.

Anderson, T., & Dron, J. (2011). Three generations of distance education pedagogy. *International Review of Research in Open and Distance Learning, 12*(3), on-line. Retrieved from http://www.irrodl.org/index.php/irrodl/article/view/890/1663

Angelo, T. (1991). Ten easy pieces: Assessing higher learning in four dimensions.

In T. Angelo (Ed.), *Classroom research: Early lessons from success, New directions for teaching and learning*, No. 46. San Francisco: Jossey-Bass.

Angelo, T. (1993). A "teachers dozen." *American Association for Higher Education Bulletin, 45* (8), 3-7, 1

Angelov, I., Menon, S., & Douma, M. (2010). Finding information: Factors that improve online experiences. In H. Yang & S. Yuen (Eds.), *Handbook of research on practices and outcomes in e-learning: Issues and trends* (pp. 493-506). Hershey, PA: IGI Publishing.

Anton-Oldenburg, M. (2002). Celebrate diversity! In K. Cauley, F. Linder, & J. McMillan (Eds.), *Annual editions: Educational psychology 02/03* (17th ed., pp. 67-69). Guilford, CT: McGraw-Hill Dushkin.

Arikan, A. (2012). Privacy concerns in social network sites. In T. Le & Q. Le (Eds.), *Technologies for enhancing pedagogy, engagement and empowerment in education: Creating learning-friendly environments* (pp. 139-146). Hershey, PA: Information Science Reference.

Aronson, J. (1987). Six keys to effective instruction in large classes: Advice from a practitioner. In M. Weimer (Ed.), *Teaching large classes well* (pp. 31-37). San Francisco: Jossey-Bass.

Arter, J. (2002). Teaching about performance assessment. In K. Cauley, F. Linder, & J. McMillan (Eds.), *Annual editions: Educational psychology 02/03* (17th ed., pp. 186-202). Guilford, CT: McGraw-Hill Dushkin.

Arvidson, P. (2008). *Teaching non-majors: Advice for liberal arts professors.* Albany, NY: State University of New York Press.

Ashton, P. (2012a). "Hearing Every Voice:" Promoting engagement through electronic discussion. In R. Morgan & K. Olivares (Eds.), *Quick hits for teaching with technology: Successful strategies by award-winning teachers* (pp. 24-25). Bloomington, IN: Indiana University Press.

Ashton, P. (2012b). Using clickers to promote participation. In R. Morgan & K. Olivares (Eds.), *Quick hits for teaching with technology: Successful strategies by award-winning teachers* (pp. 78-80). Bloomington, IN: Indiana University Press

Aslani, G., Haghani, F., Moshtaghi, S., & Zeinali, S. (2013). A comparison of the effect of presenting advanced organizers in web-based instruction. *Procedia Social and Behavioral Sciences, 83,* 200-203. Available from http://www.sciencedirect.com/science/article/pii/S1877042813010690#

Auttawutikul, S., Wiwitkunkasem, K., & Smith, D. R. (2013). Use of weblogs to enhance group learning and design creativity amongst students at a Thai University. *Innovations in Education and Teaching International, 50.* Available online from http://www.tandfonline.com/doi/full/10.1080/14703297.2013.796723#.Urd5UPuPU68

Baggio, B., & Beldarrain, Y. (2011). *Anonymity and learning in digitally mediated communications: Authenticity and trust in cyber education.* Hershey PA: Information Science Reference.

Bailey, J. (2012, December 13). *7 higher education trends for 2013.* Post University. Retrieved from http://blog.post.edu/2012/12/7-higher-education-trends-for-2013.html

Bain, K. (2004). *What the best college teachers do.* Cambridge, MA: Harvard University Press.

Ball, N. (2011). Technology in adult education ESOL classes. *Journal of Adult Education, 40*(1), 12-19. Retrieved from http://search.proquest.com/docview/917548084?accountid=14739

Banas, J. (2011). Standardized, flexible design of the electronic learning environment to enhance learning efficiency and effectiveness. In A. Kitchenham (Ed.), *Models for interdisciplinary mobile learning: Delivering information to students* (pp. 66-86). Hershey, PA: Information Science Reference.

Banks, K. (2012a). Use of SoftChalk software to create interactive content. In R. Morgan & K. Olivares (Eds.), *Quick hits for teaching with technology: Successful strategies by award-winning teachers* (pp. 83-85). Bloomington, IN: Indiana University Press.

Banks, K. (2012b). Using cartoons or short movies to engage students. In R. Morgan & K. Olivares (Eds.), *Quick hits for teaching with technology: Successful strategies by award-winning teachers* (pp. 108-110). Bloomington, IN: Indiana University Press.

Barbour, K., & Marshall, D. (2012). The academic online: Constructing persona through the World Wide Web. *First Monday, 17*(9), September 3, online. Available from http://firstmonday.org/ojs/index.php/fm/article/view/3969/3292

Barell, J. (2003). *Developing more curious minds.* Alexandria, VA: Association for Supervision and Curriculum Development.

Baron, J. (1987). Evaluating thinking skills in the classroom. In J. Baron & R. Sternberg (Eds.), *Teaching thinking skills: Theory and practice* (pp. 221-247). New York: Freeman.

Barr, R., & Tagg, J. (2004). From teaching to learning: A new paradigm for undergraduate education. Retrieved from

https://westmont.edu/_offices/institutional_portfolio/program_review/documents/FromTachingtoLearningbyBarrandTagg_000.pdf

Barrett, B., Higa, C., & Ellis, R. A. (2012). Emerging university student experiences of learning technologies across the Asia Pacific. *Computers & Education, 58*(4), 1021-1027. Available from http://www.sciencedirect.com/science/article/pii/S0360131511003022

Bates, C. (2013a). *Presentation tip: How to find creative commons & license-free photos.* Retrieved from http://carolhbates.com/presentation-tip-how-to-find_creative-commons-license-free-photos/

Bates, C. (2013b). *Preventing cheating in online classes.* Retrieved from http://carolhbates.com/preventing-cheating-in-online-classes/

Baughman, M. (1974). *Baughman's handbook of humor in education.* West Nyack, NY: Parker.

Beachem, K. (1996). Teaching needs personal style. *The Teaching Professor, 10*(10), 3.

Beckett, J. (2013, March 14). *Online learning: Will technology transform higher education?* Stanford University, Faculty of Engineering. Retrieved from http://engineering.stanford.edu/news/online-learning-will-technology-transform-higher-education

Beidler, P. (Ed.). (1986). *Distinguished teachers on effective teaching.* San Francisco: Jossey-Bass.

Beidler, P. (2011). *Risk teaching: Reflections from inside and outside the classroom.* Seattle, WA: Coffeetown Press.

Bell, R. L., Maeng, J. L., & Binns, I. C. (2013). Learning in context: Technology integration in a teacher preparation program informed by situated learning theory. *Journal of Research in Science Teaching, 50*(3), 348-379. Available from http://onlinelibrary.wiley.com/doi/10.1002/tea.21075/full

Belloni, M., & Christian, W. (2012). The Physlet project. In R. Morgan & K. Olivares (Eds.), *Quick hits for teaching with technology: Successful strategies by award-winning teachers* (pp. 54-56). Bloomington, IN: Indiana University Press.

Bennett, L., & Scholes, R. (2001). Goals and attitudes related to technology use in a social studies method course. *Contemporary Issues in Technology and Teacher Education, 1*(3), 373-385. Available from http://www.citejournal.org/vol1/iss3/currentissues/socialstudies/article1.htm

Benson, S., & Ward, C. (2013). Teaching with technology: Using TPACK to understand teaching expertise in online higher education. *Journal of Educational Computing Research, 48*(2), 153-172. Abstract available from http://punya.educ.msu.edu/2013/05/30/tpack-newsletter-issue-16-may-2013/

Bergin, J. (2001, February). A pattern language for initial course design. *ACM SIGCSE Bulletin, 33*(1), 282-286. Available from http://dl.acm.org/citation.cfm?doid=364447.364602

Bergstrom, P. (2011, June). Shifting the emphasis from teaching to learning: Process-based assessment in nurse education. *The International Review of Research in Open and Distance Learning, 12*(5). Retrieved from http://www.irrodl.org/index.php/irrodl/article/view/957/1856

Berliner, D., & Calfee, P. (Eds.). (2004). *Handbook of educational psychology* (2nd ed.). Mahwah, NJ: Lawrence Erlbaum.

Berry, B. (2011). *Teaching 2030: What we must do for our students and our public schools now and in the future.* New York: Teachers College Press.

Bibace, R., Catlin, R., Quirk, M., Beattie, K., & Slabaugh, R. (1981). Teaching styles in the faculty-resident relationship. *Journal of Family Practice, 13,* 895–900.

Biggs, J., & Tang, C. (2011). *Teaching for quality learning at university* (4th ed.). New York: McGraw-Hill International.

Blanchard, K. & Associates. (2010). *Leading at a higher level.* Upper Saddle River, NJ: Blanchard Management Corporation and FT Press.

Bloom, B., Englehart, M., Furst, E., Hill, W., & Krathwohl, D. (1956). *Taxonomy of educational objectives. Handbook 1: Cognitive domain.* New York: McKay.

Boddington, A., & Boys, J. (Eds.). (2011). *Re-shaping learning: A critical reader: The future of learning spaces in a post-compulsory education.* Rotterdam, The Netherlands: Sense Publishers.

Boggs, J., Mickel, A., & Holtom, B. (2007). Experiential learning through interactive drama: An alternative to student role plays. *Journal of Management Education, 31*(6), 832-858. doi: 10.1177/1052562906294952 Retrieved from http://www18.georgetown.edu/data/people/bch6/publication-39529.pdf

Bolliger, D., Supanakorn S., & Boggs, C. (2010). Impact of podcasting on student motivation in the online learning environment. *Computers and Education, 55,* 714-722. Retrieved from http://www.sciencedirect.com/science/article/pii/S0360131510000746

Bonwell, C. (1996). Research watch: Building a supportive climate for active learning. *The National Teaching & Learning Forum, 6*(1), 4-7.

Bork, A. (2001). What is needed for effective learning on the Internet? *Educational Technology & Society 4*(3), 139-144. Retrieved from http://www.ifets.info/journals/4_3/bork.pdf

Bowe, R. (2011). Instructional technology adoption strategies for college of education faculty. *Society for Information Technology & Teacher Education International Conference, 2011,* 1778-1785. Abstract and power-point available at http://site.aace.org/conf/site/sessions/index.cfm/fuseaction/PaperDetails?&presentation_id=50333

Boyle, J. (2013, April 24). *3 international edtech ideas that could help U.S. colleges.* Retrieved from http://edcetera.rafter.com/3-international-edtech-ideas-that-could-help-u-s-colleges/

Brandt, R. (1997). On using knowledge about our brain: A conversation with Bob Sylvester. *Educational Leadership, 54* (6), 16-19.

Breidenstein, A., Fahey, K., Glickman, C., & Hensley, F. (2012). *Leading for powerful learning: A guide for instructional leaders.* New York: Teachers College Press.

Brookfield, S. (1995). *Becoming a critically reflective teacher.* San Francisco: Jossey-Bass.

Brookfield, S. (1996). Teacher roles and teaching styles. In A. Tuijnman (Ed.), *International encyclopedia of adult education and training* (2nd ed., pp. 529-534). New York: Elsevier.

Brookfield, S. (2004). *The power of critical theory: Liberating adult learning and teaching.* San Francisco: Jossey-Bass.

Brookfield, S. (2006). *The skillful teacher: On technique, trust, and responsiveness in the classroom* (2nd ed.). San Francisco, CA: Jossey-Bass,

Brooks, R. (1987). Dealing with details in a large class. In M. Weimer (Ed.), *Teaching large classes well* (pp. 39-44). San Francisco: Jossey-Bass.

Brown, T., & Groff, A. (2011). But do they want us in their world? Evaluating the types of academic information students want through mobile and social media. In A. Kitchenham (Ed.), *Models for interdisciplinary mobile learning: Delivering information to students* (pp.49-65). Hershey, PA: Information Science Reference.

Bruffee, K. (1994). Making the most of knowledgeable peers. *Change, 26*(3), 39-44.

Bruffee, K. (1995). Sharing our toys: Cooperative learning versus collaborative learning. *Change, 27*(1), 12-18.

Burden, P., & Byrd, D. (2012). *Methods for effective teaching: Meeting the needs of all students* 6th ed.). New York: Pearson.

Burns-Sardone, N. (2008). *An investigation of the relationship between higher education learning environments and learner characteristics to the development of information technology fluency and course satisfaction.* PhD Thesis. New York: New York University. Retrieved from http://proquest.umi.com/pqdweb?did=1507558201&Fmt=7&clientId=12306&RQT=309&VName=PQD

But I made a 9 in psychology. (1996, November). *University Affairs, 37*(9), 5.

Calbraith, D., & Dennick, R., (2011). Producing generic principles and pedagogies for mobile learning. In A. Kitchenham (Ed.), *Models for interdisciplinary mobile learning: Delivering information to students* (pp.26-48). Hershey, PA: Information Science Reference.

Car, N. (2010). Is Google making us stupid? In S. Choney, *Internet making our brains different, not dumb.* msnbc.com February 19, 2010. Retrieved from http://www.msnbc.msn.com/clarnprint/CleanPrintProxy.aspx?1294090717649

Carmean, C. (2010). E-learning design for the information workplace. In H. Yang & S. Yuen (Eds.), *Handbook of research on practices and outcomes in e-learning: Issues and trends* (pp. 211-221). Hershey, PA: IGI Publishing.

Carnegie Mellon University. (n.d.). *Teaching excellence & educational innovation: Technology for education.* Eberly Center. Retrieved from http://www.cmu.edu/teaching/technology/index.html

Case, R., Harper, K., Tilley, S., & Wiens, J. (1994, Summer). Stewart on teaching versus facilitating: A misconstrued dichotomy. *Canadian Journal of Education, 19*(3), 287-298. Available at http://www.jstor.org/stable/1495133

Casey-Doecke, J. (2012). Using e-rewards to promote engagement and re-engagement in the online classroom. In R. Morgan, & K. Olivares (Eds.), *Quick hits for teaching with technology: Successful strategies by award-winning teachers* (pp. 7-8). Bloomington, IN: Indiana University Press.

Cashin, W. (1990). Improving lectures. In M. Weimer & R. Neff (Eds.), *Teaching college: Collected readings for the new instructor* (pp. 59-63). Madison, WI: Magna.

Cavin, R. (2008). Developing technological pedagogical content knowledge in pre-service teachers through microteaching lesson study. In K. McFerrin et al. (Eds.), *Proceedings of Society for Information Technology & Teacher Education International Conference, 2008* (pp. 5214-5220). Chesapeake, VA: AACE. Retrieved August 2, 2013 from http://www.editlib.org/p/28106

Chen, P. (2010). From memorable to transformative e-learning experiences: Theory and practice of experience design. In H. Yang & S. Yuen (Eds.), *Handbook of research on practices and outcomes in e-learning: Issues and trends* (pp. 402-421). Hershey, PA: IGI Publishing.

Chen, H., & Kao, C. (2012). Empirical validation of the importance of employees' learning motivation for workplace e-learning in Taiwanese organisations. *Australasian Journal of Educational Technology, 28*(4), 580-598. Retrieved from http://www.ascilite.org.au/ajet/ajet28/chen-hj.pdf

Chen, N., Lin K., & Kinshuk, (2008). Analysing users' satisfaction with e-learning using a negative critical incidents approach. *Innovations in Education and Teaching International, 45*(2), 115-120. Retrieved from http://www.tandfonline.com/doi/pdf/10.1080/14703290801950286

Cheon, J. & Grant, M. (2009). Are pretty interfaces worth the time? The effects of user interface types on web-based instruction. *Journal of Interactive Learning Research, 20*(1), 5-33. Chesapeake, VA: AACE. Retrieved from http://www.editlib.org/p/25210

Chickering, A., & Ehrmann, S. (1996, October). Implementing the seven principles: Technology as a lever. *AAHE Bulletin,* 3-6. Available at http://www.tltgroup.org/programs/seven.html

Chi-Yin Yuen, S., & Hao Yang, H. (2010). Using blog-folios to enhance interaction in e-learning courses. In H. Yang & S. Yuen (Eds.). *Handbook of research on practices and outcomes in e- learning: Issues and trends* (pp. 455-492). Hershey, PA: Information Science Reference.

Cho, C., Ramanan, R., & Feldman, M. (2011). Defining the ideal qualities of mentorship: A qualitative analysis of the characteristics of outstanding mentors. *The American Journal of Medicine, 124*(5), 453-458. Retrieved from http://www.sciencedirect.com/science/article/pii/S0002934311000088?np=y

Chou, C. (2010). Student perceptions and pedagogical applications of e-learning tools in online courses. In H. Yang & S. Yuen (Eds.). *Handbook of research on practices and outcomes in e- learning: Issues and trends* (pp. 440-454). Hershey, PA: Information Science Reference.

Christian, W., & Belloni, M. (2012). The open source physics project on Compadre. In R. Morgan & K. Olivares (Eds.), *Quick hits for teaching with technology: Successful strategies by award-winning teachers* (pp. 40-41). Bloomington, IN: Indiana University Press.

Chrosniak, P., Ralph, E., & Walker, K. (2013. February 19). What role can questioning play in mentorship? *The Mentor: An Academic Advising Journal.* Penn State University, Division of Undergraduate Studies. Available online from http://dus.psu.edu/mentor/2013/02/role-questioning-play-mentorship/

Churchill, D. (2009). Educational applications of Web 2.0: Using blogs to support teaching and learning. *British Journal of Educational Technology, 40*(1), 179-183. doi:10.1111/j.1467-8535.2008.00865.x Retrieved from http://onlinelibrary.wiley.com/doi/10.1111/j.1467-8535.2008.00865.x/full

Clegg, V., & Cashin, W. (1990). Improving multiple-choice tests. In M. Weimer & R. Neff (Eds.), *Teaching college: Collected readings for the new instructor* (pp. 125-131). Madison, WI: Magna.

Collins, R. (2011). *The role of learning styles and technology.* In E. Ng., N. Karacapilidis, & M. Raisinghani (Eds.), *Dynamic advancements in teaching and learning based technologies: New concepts* (pp. 299-315). Hershey, PA: Information Science Reference.

Columbia College. (2013). *Actions instructors can take to help prevent cheating in exams.* Retrieved from http://www.college.columbia.edu/faculty/resourcesforinstructors/academicintegrity/exam

Commons, M., Richards, F., & Armon, C. (Eds.). (1984). *Beyond formal operations: Late adolescent and adult cognitive development.* New York: Praeger.

Conole, G., & Culver, J. (2010). The design of Cloudworks: Applying social networking practice to foster the exchange of learning and teaching ideas and design. *Computers & Education, 54,* 679–692. Retrieved from http://www.sciencedirect.com/science/article/pii/S036013150900253X

Conley. M. (2012). *Content area literacy: Learners in context* (2nd ed.). Toronto: Pearson.

Conrad, R., & Donaldson, J. (2012). *Continuing to engage the online learner: More activities and resources for creative instruction.* San Francisco: Jossey-Bass.

Cook, D., Bahn, R., & Menaker, R. (2010). Speed mentoring: An innovative method to facilitate mentoring relationships. *Medical Teacher, 32*(8), 692-694. doi:10.3109/01421591003686278

Coombs, N. (2010). *Making online teaching accessible: Inclusive course design for students with disabilities.* San Francisco: John Wiley & Sons, Inc.

Cooper, P. (2012). A class wiki for the physical sciences. In R. Morgan & K. Olivares (Eds.), *Quick hits for teaching with technology: Successful strategies by award-winning teachers* (pp. 65-66). Bloomington, IN: Indiana University Press.

Cornett, C. (1983). *What you should know about teaching and learning styles* (Fastback No. 191). Bloomington, IN: Phi Delta Kappa Foundation.

Costa, A., Garmston, R., & Zimmerman, D. (2014). *Cognitive capital: Investing in teacher quality.* New York: Teachers College Press.

Coswatte, S., & Ives, K. (2013). Developing blended learning mastery. *Proceedings of the 10th Annual Sloan Consortium Blended Learning Conference and Workshop, July 8-9.* Milwaukee, WI. Retrieved from http://sloanconsortium.org/conference/2013/blended/developing-blended-learning-mastery

Coutinho, C. (2010). Challenges for teacher education in the learning society: Case studies of promising practice. In H. Yang & S. Yuen (Eds.), *Handbook of research on practices and outcomes in e-learning: Issues and trends* (pp. 385-401). Hershey, PA: IGI Publishing.

Coutinho, C., & Bottentuit, J., Jr. (2010). From Web to Web 2.0 and E-learning 2.0. In H. Yang & S. Yuen (Eds.), *Handbook of research on practices and outcomes in e-learning: Issues and trends* (pp. 19-37). Hershey, PA: IGI Publishing.

Cronin, J. (1993). Four misconceptions about authentic learning. *Educational Leadership, 50*(7), 78-80.

Cruickshank, D., & Haefele, D. (2002). Good teacers, plural. In K. Cauley, F. Linder, & J. McMillan (Eds.), *Annual editions: Educational psychology 02/03* (17th ed., pp. 8-11). Guilford, CT: McGraw-Hill Dushkin.

Curzon, L. (2004). *Teaching in further education: An outline of principles and practice* (6th ed.). London, UK: Continuum.

Dabbagha, N., & Kitsantasb, A. (2012). Personal learning environments, social media, and self-regulated learning: A natural formula for connecting formal and informal learning. *The Internet and Higher Education, 15*(1), 3–8. doi.org/10.1016/j.iheduc.2011.06.002 Retrieved from http://www.sciencedirect.com/science/article/pii/S1096751611000467

Dale, J. (2013, May 16). Are language teachers leading the way with education technology? *The Guardian: Language Learning in Focus.* Retrieved from http://www.guardian.co.uk/teacher-network/teacher-blog/2013/may/16/language-teachers-technology-social-media.

Daloz, L. (2012). *Mentor: Guiding the journey of adult learners* (2nd ed.). San Francisco: Jossey-Bass, Wiley.

Daloz, L., Keen, C., Keen, J., & Parks, S. (1996). Lives of commitment. *Change, 28*(3), 10-15.

Dalziel, C., & Poot, A. (2011). ePortfolio based assessment strategies to prevent plagiarism. In J. Yorke (Ed.), *Meeting the challenges. Proceedings of the ATN (Australian Technology Network) Assessment Conference,* 20-21 October (p. 23). Perth, Western Australia: Curtin University. Retrieved from http://otl.curtin.edu.au/professional_development/conferences/atna2011/files/ATNA_2011_Proceedings.pdf

Danielson, C. (2007). *Enhancing professional practice: A framework for teaching* (2nd ed.). Alexandria, VA: Association for Supervision and Curriculum Development.

Danish, J. (2012). Designing authentic cross-class collaboration by focusing on activity. In R. Morgan & K. Olivares (Eds.), *Quick hits for teaching with technology: Successful strategies by award-winning teachers* (pp. 26-28). Bloomington, IN: Indiana University Press.

Davidson, C., & Ambrose, S. (1995). Leading discussions effectively. *The Teaching Professor, 9*(6), 8.

Davies, S. (2010). *Effective assessment in a digital age: A guide to technology-enhanced assessment and feedback.* Bristol, UK: Joint Information Systems Committee. Retrieved from http://www.jisc.ac.uk/media/documents/programmes/elearning/digiassass_eada.pdf

Davis, G. (2014). Do calculators interfere with students' learning of mathematics? *Saskatchewan Bulletin, 80*(6), 6. Saskatoon, Saskatchewan, Canada: Saskatchewan Teachers Federation.

Davis, H. C., & Fill, K. (2007). Embedding blended learning in a university's teaching culture: Experiences and reflections. *British Journal of Educational Technology, 38*(5), 817-828. Available at http://onlinelibrary.wiley.com/doi/10.1111/j.1467-8535.2007.00756.x/full

de Charms, R. (1984). Motivation enhancement in educational settings. In R. Ames & C. Ames (Eds.), *Research on motivation in education: Vol. 1. Student motivation* (pp. 275-310). Toronto, ON: Academic.

Dembo, M. (2013). *Motivation and learning strategies for college success: A self-management approach* (3rd ed.). New York: Routledge.

Dennis, A., Fuller, R., & Valacich, J. (2008). Media, tasks, and communication processes: A theory of media synchronicity. *MIS Quarterly, 32*(3), 575-600.

De Wever, B., Van Keer, H., Schellens, T., & Valcke, M. (2009). Structuring asynchronous discussion groups: The impact of role assignment and self-assessment on students' levels of knowledge construction through social negotiation. *Journal of Computer Assisted Learning, 25*(2), 177-188. Retrieved from http://onlinelibrary.wiley.com/doi/10.1111/j.1365-2729.2008.00292.x/full

Dill, D. D. (2000). Is there an academic audit in your future? Reforming quality assurance in US higher education. *Change: The Magazine of Higher Learning, 32*(4), 34-41.

Dillon, J. (1983). *Teaching and the art of questioning* (Fastback No. 194). Bloomington, IN: Phi Delta Kappa Foundation.

Dillon, R., & Sternberg, R. (Eds.). (1986). *Cognition and instruction.* New York: Academic.

Dixson, M. (2012a). Grading discussion forums in the online environment. In R. Morgan & K. Olivares (Eds.), *Quick hits for teaching with technology: Successful strategies by award-winning teachers* (pp. 67-68). Bloomington, IN: Indiana University Press.

Dixson, M. (2012b). Using team-based learning to engage students in online courses. In R. Morgan & K. Olivares (Eds.), *Quick hits for teaching with technology: Successful strategies by award-winning teachers* (pp. 11-13). Bloomington, IN: Indiana University Press.

Doyle, D. (1997). Education and character: A constructive view. *Phi Delta Kappan, 78*(6), 440-443.

Doyle, T. (2008). *Helping students learn in a learner-centered environment: A guide to facilitating learning in higher education.* Sterling, VA: Stylus Jossey-Bass.

Draves, W. (2007). *How to teach adults* (3rd ed.). River Falls, WI: Learning Resources Network.

Driscoll, M. (2009). *Psychology of learning for instruction* (4th ed.). Boston: Allyn and Bacon.

Dror, I. (2011). *Technology enhanced learning and cognition.* Philadelphia: John Benjamins.

Du, J., Liu, Y., & Brown, R. (2010). The key elements of online learning communities. In H. Yang & S. Yuen (Eds.), *Handbook of research on practices and outcomes in e-learning: Issues and trends* (pp. 61-74). Hershey, PA: IGI Publishing.

Ducharme, E. (2012). The great teacher question: Beyond competencies. In K. Ryan & J. Cooper (Eds.), *Kaleidoscope: Contemporary and classic readings in education* (13th ed., Chapter 1). Independence, KY: Cengage Wadsworth.

Duffy, T. & Rimmer, R. (2008). *Improving students' motivation to study A photocopiable resource for college and university lecturers.* Devon, UK: Reflect Press.

Dunlap, J. C., & Lowenthal, P. R. (2011). Learning, unlearning, and relearning: Using Web 2.0 technologies to support the development of lifelong learning skills. In G. D. Magoulas (Ed.), *E-infrastructures and technologies for lifelong learning: Next generation environments.* Hershey, PA: IGI Global.

Dunn, J. (2013, May 28). New padagogy [sic] wheel helps you integrate technology using SAMR model. *Edudemic.* Retrieved from http://www.edudemic.com/2013/05/new-padagogy-wheel-helps-you-integrate-technology-using-samr-model/

Dunning, J. (2014, February 25). Live chat: Youth obsession with technology [Web log post on *CBC Community Blog*]. Retrieved from http://www.cbc.ca/newsblogs/yourcommunity/2014/02/live-chat-youth-obsession-with-technology.html

Dwaraka, A. (2013, May 16). 5 tested ways to motivate adult learners in e-learning [Web log post on *CommLabIndia*]. Retrieved from http://blog.commlabindia.com/elearning/motivating-learners-in-elearning

Dweck, C. (2002). Messages that motivate: How praise molds students' beliefs, motivation, and performance (in surprising ways). In J. Aronson (Ed.), *Improving academic achievement: Impact of psychological factors on education* (pp. 37-59). Cambridge, MA: Elsevier.

Eble, K. (1994). *The craft of teaching: A guide to mastering the professor's art* (2nd ed.). San Francisco: Jossey-Bass

Edgerton, R. (1996). Learning, teaching, technology: Putting first things first. *American Association for Higher Education Bulletin, 49*(1), 3-6.

Education in America. (2013). *Four ways educators use classroom humor as a teaching tool.* Author, Hot chalk. Retrieved from http://www.educationinamerica.com/blog/four-ways-educators-use-classroom-humor-as-a-teaching-tool/

Eggen, P., & Kauchak, D. (2012). *Educational psychology: Windows on classrooms* (9th ed.).Toronto, ON: Pearson Merrill/Prentice Hall

Eichinger, R., & Lombardo, M. (2003). *Education competencies: Humor.* Microsoft in education/training. Retrieved from http://www.microsoft.com/education/en-us/Training/Competencies/Pages/humor.aspx

Elliott, S., Katochwill, T., & Littlefield Cook, J. (2000). *Educational psychology: Effective teaching, effective learning* (3rd ed.). Whitby, ON: McGraw-Hill Ryerson.

Ellis Ormrod, J., Saklofske, D., Schwean, V., Harrison G., & Andrews J. (2006). *Principles of educational psychology* (Canadian Ed.). Toronto, ON: Pearson.

Ellison, N., & Wu, Y. (2008). Blogging in the classroom: A preliminary exploration of student attitudes and impact on comprehension. *Journal of Educational Multimedia and Hypermedia, 17*(1), 99-122. Chesapeake, VA: AACE. Retrieved from http://www.editlib.org/p/24310.

Elzarka, S. (2012). *Technology use in higher education instruction* (Doctoral dissertation, Claremont Graduate University). Retrieved from http://scholarship.claremont.edu/cgi/viewcontent.cgi?article=1039&context=cgu_etd

Evans, N. (1994). *Experiential learning for all.* London: Cassell.

Fan, S., & Le, Q. (2012). Web-based learning: Status quo and trend. In T. Le & Q. Le (Eds.), *Technologies for enhancing pedagogy, engagement and empowerment in education: Creating learning-friendly environments* (pp. 217-230). Hershey, PA: Information Science Reference.

Feldman, M. D., Arean, P. A., Marshall, S. J., Lovett, M., & O'Sullivan, P. (2010). Does mentoring matter: Results from a survey of faculty mentees at a large health sciences university. *Medical Education Online, 15*(5063). Retrieved from http://www.ncbi.nlm.nih.gov/pmc/articles/PMC2860862/

Felver, L. (2012). Online art galleries and clinical stories. In R. Morgan & K. Olivares (Eds.), *Quick hits for teaching with technology: Successful strategies by award-winning teachers* (pp. 31-32). Bloomington, IN: Indiana University Press.

Feng, J., Shih, M., Kao, C. P., & Tsai, C. C. (2011). A study of university students' learning conceptions and approaches of web-searching bases on the disciplinary differences. In T. Bastiaens & M. Ebner (Eds.), *Proceedings of World Conference on Educational Multimedia, Hypermedia and Telecommunications, 2011*(pp. 2187-2189). Retrieved from http://www.editlib.org/p/38163

Feng, P. (2012). Blogging in the classroom. In R. Morgan & K. Olivares (Eds.), *Quick hits for teaching with technology: Successful strategies by award-winning teachers* (pp. 48-49). Bloominton, IN: Indiana University Press.

Fidishun, D. (n.d.). *Andragogy and technology: Integrating adult learning theory as we teach with technology.* Retrieved from http://frank.mtsu.edu/~itconf/proceed00/fidishun.htm

Fiedor, L. (2012). Social engagement. In R. Morgan & K. Olivares (Eds.), *Quick hits for teaching with technology: Successful strategies by award-winning teachers* (pp. 29-31). Bloomington, IN: Indiana University Press.

Filene, P. (2005) *The joy of teaching: A practical guide for new college instructors*. Chapel Hill, NC: The University of North Carolina Press.

Foundation for Critical Thinking, Critical Thinking Community. (2011). *An overview of how to design instruction using critical thinking concepts*. Retrieved from http://www.criticalthinking.org/pages/an-overview-of-how-to-design-instruction-using-critical-thinking-concepts/439

Foster, J. (2006). Scaling issues associated with using classroom technologies. *Proceedings of the Canadian Engineering Education Association*. Abstract available at http://library.queensu.ca/ojs/index.php/PCEEA/article/view/3815

Foster, K. (2014, March 28). The psychology of cheating is never black and white. On Campus News, 21 (14), 8, 11. Retrieved from http://words.usask.ca/news/files/OCN_Mar28_web.pdf

Frazee, B., & Rudnitski, R. (1995). *Integrated teaching methods*. Boston, MA: Delmar.

Frederick, P. (1987). Student involvement: Active learning in large classes. In M. Weimer (Ed.), *Teaching large classes well* (pp. 45-56). San Francisco: Jossey-Bass.

Freiberg, H., & Driscoll, A. (2000). *Universal teaching strategies* (3rd ed.).Boston: Allyn and Bacon.

Friberg, J. (2012). Using i-pad technologies to support teaching and learning in CSD (Communication Sciences & Disorders). *Perspectives on Issues in Higher Education, 15*(2), 16-21. doi:10.1044/ihe15.2.51

Fried, C. (2008). In-class laptop use and its effects on student learning. *Computers & Education, 50,* 906-914. doi:10.1016/j.compedu.2006.09.006 Retrieved from http://www.sciencedirect.com/science/article/pii/S0360131506001436

Frith, C. (n.d.). *Motivation to learn*. Department of Educational Communications and Technology, University of Saskatchewan, Saskatoon, Saskatchewan, Canada. Retrieved from http://www.usask.ca/education/coursework/802papers/Frith/Motivation.PDF

Fullan, M. (2012). *Stratosphere: Integrating technology, pedagogy, and change knowledge*. Toronto, ON: Pearson.

Fullan, M. (2013, April 11). *Motion leadership in action*. Workshop at Halifax Marriott Harbourfront Hotel. Retrieved from http://www.michaelfullan.ca/images/handouts/13_Halifax_MLinAction.pdf

Fusco, E. (2012). *Effective questioning strategies in the classroom.* New York: Teachers College Press.

Gacio Harrolle, M. (2012a). Building a sense of community in an online environment: student autobiographical videos. In R. Morgan & K. Olivares (Eds.), *Quick hits for teaching with technology: Successful strategies by award-winning teachers* (pp. 30-31). Bloomington, IN: Indiana University Press.

Gacio Harrolle, M. (2012b). Personal sales pitch: Video assignment. In R. Morgan & K. Olivares (Eds.), *Quick hits for teaching with technology: Successful strategies by award-winning teachers* (pp. 76-77). Bloomington, IN: Indiana University Press.

Gagné, R., & Wager, M. (2002). *Principles of instructional design* (5th ed.). Belmont, CA: Wadsworth.

Galbraith, M., & Jones, M. (2010). Understanding incivility in online teaching. *Journal of Adult Education, 39*(2), 1-10. Retrieved from http://search.proquest.com/docview/871911644?accountid=14739

Gappa-Levi, L. (1996). TA forum: Isn't teaching drama? *The National Teaching & Learning Forum, 5*(4), 8-9.

Garavan, T., Carbery, R., O'Malley, G., & O'Donnell, D. (2010). Understanding participation in e-learning in organizations: A large-scale empirical study of employees. *International Journal of Training and Development, 14*(3), 155-168. Retrieved from http://onlinelibrary.wiley.com/doi/10.1111/j.1468-2419.2010.00349.x/pdf

Gardner, H. (1983). *Frames of mind: The theory of multiple intelligences.* New York: Basic Books.

Gardner, H. (Ed.). (1993). *Multiple intelligences: The theory in practice.* New York: Basic Books.

Gardner, H. (2000). *Intelligence reframed: Multiple intelligences for the 21st century.* New York: Basic Books.

Gardner, H. (2004). *Changing minds: The art and science of changing our own and other people's minds.* Boston, MA: Harvard Business School Press.

Garmston, R. (1994). The persuasive art of presenting: Presenting to groups experiencing change. *Journal of Staff Development, 15*(1), 66-68.

Garner, R. (2006). Humor in pedagogy. *Journal of College Teaching, 54* (1), 177-180.

Garrison, D., & Kanuka, H. (2004). Blended learning: Uncovering its transformative potential in higher education. *The Internet and Higher Education, 7*(2), 95–105. http://dx.doi.org/10.1016/j.iheduc.2004.02.001 Retrieved from http://www.sciencedirect.com/science/article/pii/S1096751604000156

Gates, Bill and Melinda, Foundation. (2009). *Background: Technology in post-secondary success*. Retrieved from http://docs.gatesfoundation.org/united-states/documents/technology-in-postsecondary-success.pdf

Gavrin, A. (2012a). Images for education— Crime free! In R. Morgan & K. Olivares (Eds.), *Quick hits for teaching with technology: Successful strategies by award-winning teachers* (pp. 92-93). Bloomington, IN: Indiana University Press.

Gavrin, A. (2012b). Just-in-time teaching: Using the web to engage students in the classroom. In R. Morgan & K. Olivares (Eds.), *Quick hits for teaching with technology: Successful strategies by award-winning teachers* (pp. 19-20). Bloomington, IN: Indiana University Press.

Gibbs, G. (1995). Promoting excellent teaching is harder than you'd think. *Change, 27*(3), 17-20.

Gibbs G., & Coffey, M. (2004). The impact of training of university teachers on their teaching skills, their approach to teaching and the approach to learning of their students. *Active Learning in Higher Education, 5*(1), 87-100. doi: 10.1177/1469787404040463 Retrieved from http://alh.sagepub.com/content/5/1/87.full.pdf+html

Gill, A. (2012, December 13th).*Technology and higher education in 2013*. LearnHub. Retrieved from http://learnhubmarketing.com/2012/12/technology-and-higher-education-in-2013/

Gillies, R. (2012). Developing medical education teaching applications for mobile devices. In R. Morgan & K. Olivares (Eds.), *Quick hits for teaching with technology: Successful strategies by award-winning teachers* (p. 46). Bloomington, IN: Indiana University Press.

Ginsberg, M., & Wlodkowski, R. (2009). Professional learning to promote motivation and academic performance among diverse adults. *CAEL Forum and News, November*, 23-32. Retrieved from http://raymondwlodkowski.com/Materials/ProfessionalLearning.pdf

Glancy, F., & Isenberg, S. (2011, May 30-31). A conceptual e-learning framework. *Proceedings of European, Mediterranean & Middle Eastern Conference on Information Systems* (pp. 636-650). Athens, Greece. Retrieved from http://www.iseing.org/emcis/EMCISWebsite/EMCIS2011%20Proceedings/ELKM2.pdf

Goering, B. (2012). "It's a small world after all:" Using technology to internationalize curriculum. In R. Morgan & K. Olivares (Eds.), *Quick hits for teaching with technology: Successful strategies by award-winning teachers* (pp. 52-53). Bloomington, IN: Indiana University Press.

Gom, O. (2009). Motivation and adult learning. *Contemporary PNG Studies: DWU Research Journal, 10,* 17-25. Retrieved from http://search.informit.com.au/documentSummary;dn=962884090077237;res=IELIND

Good, T. (1990). Building the knowledge base of teaching. In D. Dill and associates (Eds.), *What teachers need to know: The knowledge, skills, and values essential to good teaching* (pp. 17-75). San Francisco: Jossey-Bass.

Gordon, L. (2013, May 2). Using technology to fight cheating in online education. *Los Angeles Times, Phys.org.* Retrieved from http://phys.org/news/2013-05-technology-online.html

Gorges, J., & Kandler, C. (2012). Learning and individual differences. *Adult Learning, 22*(5), 610–617. Retrieved from http://www.sciencedirect.com/science/article/pii/S1041608011001804

Graf, S., & Liu, T. C. (2009). Supporting teachers in identifying students' learning styles in learning management systems: An automatic student modelling approach. *Educational Technology & Society, 12*(4), 3-14. Available at http://ca.yhs4.search.yahoo.com/r/_ylt=AwrTccBjmbdSoDkALNwXFwx.;_ylu=X3oDMTByaDNhc2JxBHNlYwNzcgRwb3MDMQRjb2xvA2dxMQR2dGlkAw--/SIG=11tj977o2/EXP=1387792867/**http%3a//www.ifets.info/journals/12_4/2.pdf

Graham, S., & Weiner, B. (2012). Motivation: Past, present, and future. In K. Harris, S. Graham, & T. Urban (Eds.), *APA educational psychology handbook, Volume 1: Theories, constructs, and critical issues* (pp. 367-397). Washington, DC: American Psychological Association

Grajek, S. (2013, June 3). Top-ten IT issues, 2013: Welcome to the connected age. *Educause Review Online.* Retrieved from http://www.educause.edu/ero/article/top-ten-it-issues-2013-welcome-connected-age

Grasha, A. (1996). *Teaching with style: A practical guide to enhancing learning by understanding teaching and learning styles.* Pittsburgh, PA: Alliance. Retrieved from http://www.ius.edu/ilte/pdf/teaching_with_style.pdf

Grasha, A., & Yangarber-Hicks, N. (2000). Integrating teaching styles and learning styles with instructional technology. *College Teaching, 48*(1), 2-10.

Grasha-Riechmann Student Learning Style Scales (GRSLSS, n.d.). Retrieved from http://www.ccsonline.ca/Resources/ideas/grasha-riechmann_learning_styles.pdf

Greer, A., & Mott, V. (2011). Learner-centered teaching and the use of technology. In E. Ng., N. Karacapilidis, & M. Raisinghani (Eds.), *Dynamic advancements in teaching and learning based technologies: New concepts* (pp. 248-263). Hershey, PA: Information Science Reference.

Gross Davis, B. (2009). *Tools for teaching* (2nd ed.). New York: John Wiley.

Guertin, L. (2012). Utilizing existing gigapixel panoramas for virtual fieldtrips. In R. Morgan & K. Olivares (Eds.), *Quick hits for teaching with technology: Successful strategies by award-winning teachers* (p. 43). Bloomington, IN: Indiana University Press

Guest Writer. (2012, August 21). 50 education technology tools every teacher should know about. *Edumedia.* Retrieved from http://www.edudemic.com/2012/08/50-education-technology-tools-every-teacher-should-know-about/

Guhlin, M. (2009). Eight tips for successful online course facilitation. *Education World on-line.* Retrieved from http://www.educationworld.com/a_tech/columnists/guhlin/guhlin014.shtml

Gururajan, R., Hafeez-Baig, A., Danaher, P., & De George-Walker, L. (2011). Student perceptions and uses of wireless handheld devices: Implications for implementing blended and mobile learning in an Australian university. In A. Kitchenham (Ed.), *Models for interdisciplinary mobile learning: Delivering information to students* (pp. 231-246). Hershey, PA: Information Science Reference.

Guskey, T. (1996). Reporting on student learning: Lessons from the past--prescriptions for the future. In T. Guskey (Ed.), *Communicating student learning* (pp. 13-24). Alexandria, VA: Association for Supervision and Curriculum Development.

Guzzetti, B., Elliott, K., & Welsch, D. (2010). *DIY media in the classroom: New literacies across content areas.* New York: Teachers College Press.

Hagner, P. R. (2000). Interesting practices and best systems in faculty engagement and support. *Education, 35*(5), 1-32. Available at http://ca.yhs4.search.yahoo.com/r/_ylt=AwrTcctXm7dSX3kA4P0XFwx.;_ylu=X3oDMTByaDNhc2JxBHNlYwNzcgRwb3MDMQRjb2xvA2dxMQR2dGlkAw--/SIG=126d1f0rr/EXP=1387793367/**http%3a//net.educause.edu/ir/library/pdf/NLI0017.pdf

Hall, C., & Lowe, M. (2014, January 21). Best phablets 2014: The best big-screened phones to buy right now. *Pocket-lint Ltd. online.* Retrieved from http://www.pocket-lint.com/news/124518-best-phablets-2014-the-best-big-screened-phones-to-buy-right-now

Hanewald, R., & Ng, W. (2011). The digital revolution in education: Digital citizenship and multi-literacy of mobile technology. In W. Ng (Ed.), *Mobile technologies and handheld devices for ubiquitous learning: Research and pedagogy* (pp. 1-14). Hershey, PA: Information Science Reference.

Harasim, L. M. (2012). *Learning theory and online technologies.* New York: Routledge.

Harrington, C. (2013, April 16). Online quizzing to promote learning: A formative assessment approach. *Cengage Learning.* Retrieved from http://blog.cengage.com/?top_blog=online-quizzing-to-promote-learning-a-formative-assessment-approach

Harris, J., & Hofer, M. (2011). Technological pedagogical content knowledge (TPACK) in action: A descriptive study of secondary teachers' curriculum-based, technology-related instructional planning. *Journal of Research on Technology in Education, 43*(3), 211. Available at http://eric.ed.gov/?q=Harris%2c+J.%2c+%26+Hofer%2c+M.+(2011).+Technological+pedagogical+content+knowledge+(TPACK)+in+action%3a+A+descriptive+study+of+secondary+teachers%27+curriculum-based%2c+technology-related+instructional+planning.+Journal+of+Research+on+Technology+in+Education%2c+43(3)%2c+211.&id=EJ918905

Hartshorne, R., Ajjan, H., & Ferdig, R. (2010). Faculty use and perceptions of Web 2.0 in higher education. In H. Yang, & S. Yuen (Eds.), H*andbook of Research on Practices and Outcomes in E-Learning: Issues and Trends* (pp. 241-259). Hershey, PA: IGI Publishing.

Hattie, J., & Yates, G. (2013). *Visible learning and the science of how we learn.* New York: Routledge.

Heick, T. (2013, May 5). What your online habits say about your teaching. *Edudemic.* Retrieved from http://edudemic.com/2013/05/what-your-online-habits-say-about-your-teaching/

Heller, N. (2013, May 20). Laptop U: Has the future of college moved online? *The New Yorker (Annals of Higher Education).* Retrieved from http://www.newyorker.com/reporting/2013/05/20/130520fa_fact_heller?currentPage=al 1

Heller, R., & Procter, M. (2011). Animated pedagogical agents: The effect of visual information on a historical figure application. In E. Ng., N. Karacapilidis, & M. Raisinghani (Eds.), *Dynamic advancements in teaching and learning based technologies: New concepts* (pp. 66-78). Hershey, PA: Information Science Reference.

Herman, J., Aschbacher, P., & Winters, L. (1992). *A practical guide to alternative assessment.* Alexandria, VA: Association for Supervision and Curriculum Development.

Hernandez-Gantes, V. (2011). The role of adult education in online delivery of career and technical education. In E. Ng., N. Karacapilidis, & M. Raisinghani (Eds.), *Dynamic advancements in teaching and learning based technologies: New concepts* (pp. 280-298). Hershey, PA: Information Science Reference.

Herold, D. (2010). Mediating media studies: Stimulating critical awareness in a virtual environment. *Computers and Education, 54,* 791-798. Retrieved from http://www.sciencedirect.com/science/article/pii/S0360131509003091

Hickerson, C., & Giglio, M. (2009). Instant messaging between students and faculty: A tool for increasing student-faculty interaction. *International Journal on E-Learning, 8(*1), 71-88. Chesapeake, VA: AACE. Retrieved August 3, 2013 from http://www.editlib.org/p/25264.

Hidi, S., Renninger, K., & Krapp, A. (1992). The present state of interest research. In K. Renninger, S. Hidi, & A. Krapp (Eds.), *The role of interest in learning and development* (pp. 433-446). Hillsdale, NJ: Laurence Erlbaum.

Hofstetter, F. (2012). Using web-based videoconferencing to extend the f2f experience to distance learners. In R. Morgan & K. Olivares (Eds.), *Quick hits for teaching with technology: Successful strategies by award-winning teachers* (pp. 57-58). Bloomington, IN: Indiana University Press.

Hoofnagle, W. M. (2012). Technology in the university and the death of Socrates. *Literature Compass, 9*(12), 1010-1015. Available from http://onlinelibrary.wiley.com/doi/10.1111/lic3.12013/full

Hope, J. (2011). What can we learn from the past about future technological trends in adult education? In E. Ng., N. Karacapilidis, & M. Raisinghani (Eds.), *Dynamic advancements in teaching and learning based technologies: New concepts* (pp. 333-353). Hershey, PA: Information Science Reference.

How the digital age affects cheating and plagiarism. (2013, April 27). *The Higher Education.* Retrieved from http://www.lsbu-multimedia-journalists.co.uk/weke/

Howles, T. (2007). Preliminary results of a longitudinal study of computer science student trends, behaviors and preferences. *Journal of Computing Sciences in Colleges, 22*(6), 18-27. Available at http://dl.acm.org/ft_gateway.cfm?id=1231097&ftid=409465&dwn=1&CFID=273258956&CFTOKEN=10776694

Hsu J., & Hamilton K. (2010). Adult learners, e-learning, and success: Critical issues and challenges. In H. Yang & S. Yuen (Eds.), *Handbook of research on practices and outcomes in e-learning: Issues and trends* (pp. 116-137). Hershey, PA: IGI Publishing.

Huang, W., Yoo, S., & Choi, J. (2008). Correlating college students' learning styles and how they use Web 2.0 applications for learning. In C. Bonk et al. (Eds.), *Proceedings of World Conference on E-Learning in Corporate, Government, Healthcare, and Higher Education, 2008* (pp. 2752-2759). Chesapeake, VA: AACE. Retrieved August 2, 2013 from http://www.editlib.org/p/30056.

Hubball, H., Clarke, A., & Poole, G. (2010). Ten-year reflections on mentoring SoTL research in a research-intensive university. *International Journal for Academic Development, 15*(2), 117-129. Available from http://ca.yhs4.search.yahoo.com/r/_ylt=AwrTcd2inLdSYRMA7eYXFwx.;_ylu=X3oDMTByc25qcnVyBHNlYwNzcgRwb3MDNARjb2xvA2dxMQR2dGlkAw--/SIG=1287c6rvr/EXP=1387793698/**http%3a//www.cte.hawaii.edu/handouts/SoTL/IJAD2010.pdf

Hunter-Rainey, S. (2012). Combining learning communities with electronic self and peer assessments to increase student engagement in discussion-based courses. In R. Morgan & K. Olivares (Eds.), *Quick hits for teaching with technology: Successful strategies by award-winning teachers* (pp. 21-22). Bloomington, IN: Indiana University Press.

Hurd, A., Beggs, B., & Elkins, D. (2011). Using online discussion boards for senior internships. *Schole: A Journal of Leisure Studies and Recreation Education, 26*(2). Abstract available at http://js.sagamorepub.com/schole/article/view/2425

Hurn, J. (2012). The inverted hybrid science classroom. In R. Morgan & K. Olivares (Eds.), *Quick hits for teaching with technology: Successful strategies by award-winning teachers* (p. 54). Bloomington, IN: Indiana University Press.

Huston, J. (1997). The details of discussion. *The Teaching Professor, 11*(2), 3.

Hyerle, D. (1996). *Visual tools for constructing knowledge.* Alexandria, VA: Association for Supervision and Curriculum Development.

Iiyoshi, T. (2013). Opportunity is knocking: Will education open the door? *Carnegie Perspectives.* Carnegie Foundation for the Advancement of Teaching. Retrieved from http://www.carnegiefoundation.org/perspectives/opportunity-knocking-will-education-open-door

Jackson, Y. (2011). *The pedagogy of confidence: Inspiring high intellectual performance in urban schools.* New York: Teachers College Press.

Jarrett Thoms, K. (n.d.). *They're not just big kids: Motivating adult learners.* Retrieved from http://frank.mtsu.edu/~itconf/proceed01/22.pdf

Jarvis, P. (2006). *Towards a comprehensive theory of adult learning.* London, UK: Routledge.

Jefferies, A., & Skidmore, M. (2010). Evaluation of a collaborative mentorship program in a multi-site postgraduate training program. *Medical Teacher, 32*(8), 695-697. doi:10.3109/01421591003692680

Johansson-Fua, S., Sanga K., Walker, K., & Ralph, E. (2011). Mentorship in the professions: A perspective from Tonga. *The International Journal of Mentoring and Coaching, 9*(2), 19-37. Retrieved from http://repository.usp.ac.fj/5376/1/Edwin_Ralph_-_Mentorship_in_the_Professions._A_Perspective_from_Tonga.pdf

Johansson-Fua, S., Ruru, D., Sanga, K., Walker, K., & Ralph, E. (2012). Creating mentorship metaphors: Pacific Island perspectives. *Learning Landscapes, 6*(1), 243-261. Available from http://repository.usp.ac.fj/5579/1/Creating_Mentorship_Metaphors_Pacific_Island_Perspectives.pdf

Jones. E. (2012). Doppelgänger Professor: High-touch delivery to low-density populations. In R. Morgan & K. Olivares (Eds.), *Quick hits for teaching with technology: Successful strategies by award-winning teachers* (pp. 59-60). Bloomington, IN: Indiana University Press.

Joyce, B., Weil, M., & Calhoun, E. (2009). *Models of teaching* (8th ed.). Boston, MA: Allyn & Bacon, Pearson.

Joyner, F. (2012). Coupling visual metaphors with discussion forums to enhance reflection and inquiry. In R. Morgan & K. Olivares (Eds.), *Quick hits for teaching with technology: Successful strategies by award-winning teachers* (pp. 103-105). Bloomington, IN: Indiana University Press.

Kahan Kennedy, C., & Hinkley, M. (2011). An evaluation of blending technology with pedagogy for teaching educators and its implication for their classroom teaching. In E. Ng., N. Karacapilidis, & M. Raisinghani (Eds.), *Dynamic advancements in teaching and learning based technologies: New concepts* (pp. 162-179). Hershey, PA: Information Science Reference.

Kalén, S., Stenfors-Hayes, T., Hylin, U., Larm, M., Hindbeck, H., & Ponzer, S. (2010). Mentoring medical students during clinical courses: A way to enhance professional development. *Medical Teacher, 32*(8), e315-e321. doi:10.3109/01421591003695295

Kalota, F., & Hung, W. C. (2013). Instructional effects of a performance support system designed to guide preservice teachers in developing technology integration strategies. *British Journal of Educational Technology, 44*(3), 442-452. Available at http://onlinelibrary.wiley.com/doi/10.1111/j.1467-8535.2012.01318.x/full

Kates, R. (2012). Creating with intentionality: Using a personal multimedia narrative to emphasize writing process. In R. Morgan & K. Olivares (Eds.), *Quick hits for teaching with technology: Successful strategies by award-winning teachers* (pp. 25-26). Bloomington, IN: Indiana University Press.

Kaufman, J. (2009). *Creativity 101*. New York: Springer.

Kelly, E. (1976). *Dramatics in the classroom: Making lessons come alive* (Fastback No. 70). Bloomington, IN: Phi Delta Kappa Educational Foundation.

Kember, D., & McNaught, C. (2007). *Enhancing university teaching lessons from research into award-winning teachers*. London, UK: Routledge.

Kennedy, K., Boyer, J., Cavanaugh, C., & Dawson, K. (2010). Student-centered teaching with constructionist technology tools: Preparing 21st century teachers. In H. Yang & S. Yuen (Eds.), *Handbook of research on practices and outcomes in e-learning: Issues and trends* (pp. 367-384). Hershey, PA: IGI Publishing.

Keogh, K. (2011). Using mobile phones for teaching, learning and assessing Irish in Ireland: Processes, benefits and challenges. In W. Ng (Ed.), *Mobile technologies and handheld devices for ubiquitous learning: Research and pedagogy* (pp. 237-258). Hershey, PA: Information Science Reference.

Kilbane, C., & Milman, N. (2014). *Teaching models: Designing instruction for 21st century learners*. Toronto, ON: Pearson.

Kilty, T. (2013). Mobile devices, field and lab experiences, and a science lab credit into the blender. *Proceedings of the 10th Annual Sloan Consortium Blended Learning Conference and Workshop, July 8-9*. Milwaukee, WI. Retrieved from http://sloanconsortium.org/conference/2013/blended/mobile-devices-field-and-lab-experiences-and-science-lab-credit-blender

King, A. (1993). From sage on the stage to guide on the side. *College Teaching, 41*(1), 30-35.

King, D. (2012). Using multiple-response clicker questions to identify student misunderstanding. In R. Morgan & K. Olivares (Eds.), *Quick hits for teaching with technology: Successful strategies by award-winning teachers* (p. 66-67). Bloomington, IN: Indiana University Press.

Kitchenham, A. (2011). Mobile learning in action: Three case studies with the net generation. In A. Kitchenham (Ed.), *Models for interdisciplinary mobile learning: Delivering information to students* (pp.104-136). Hershey, PA: Information Science Reference.

Knapper, C. (2004, May). *Research on college teaching and learning: Applying what we know*. Retrieved from http://www.stlhe.ca/wp-content/uploads/2011/07/Research-on-College-Teaching-and-Learning.pdf

Knowles, M., Holton, E., III, & Swanson, R. (2005). *The adult learner: The definitive classic in adult education and human resource development* (6th ed.). Burlington, MA: Elsevier

Kohn, A. (1997). How not to teach values: A critical look at character education. *Phi Delta Kappan, 78*(6), 428-439.

Kolb, A., & Kolb, D. (2005). *The Kolb learning style inventory–version 3.1 2005 technical specifications*. Boston, MA: Hay Resource Direct. Available at http://ca.yhs4.search.yahoo.com/r/_ylt=AwrTceDXn7dSBS4AZyAXFwx.;_ylu=X3oDMTByaDNhc2JxBHNlYwNzcgRwb3MDMQRjb2xvA2dxMQR2dGlkAw--/SIG=12np0en7c/EXP=1387794519/**http%3a//www.whitewater-rescue.com/support/pagepics/lsitechmanual.pdf

Kolovou, T. (2012). "Guest cam" in the classroom: Making speeches real. In R. Morgan & K. Olivares (Eds.), *Quick hits for teaching with technology: Successful strategies by award-winning teachers* (pp. 73-74). Bloomington, IN: Indiana University Press.

Kortecamp, K., & Croninger, W. (1996). Addressing barriers to technology diffusion. *Journal of Information Technology for Teacher Education, 5*(1-2), 71-82.

Kounin, J. (1970). *Discipline and group management in classrooms.* New York: Holt, Rinehart and Winston.

Kraft, R. (1990). Group-inquiry turns passive students active. In M. Weimer & R. Neff (Eds.), *Teaching college: Collected readings for the new instructor* (pp. 99-104). Madison, WI: Magna.

Krathwohl, D. (2002, Autumn). A revision of Bloom's taxonomy: An overview. *Theory into Practice, 41*(4), 212-264. Retrieved from http://www.unco.edu/cetl/sir/stating_outcome/documents/Krathwohl.pdf

Kumar, S. (2012). The Net generation's informal and educational use of new technologies. *In Education, 16*(1), 19-32. Available at http://ourspace.uregina.ca/bitstream/handle/10294/3098/ie16%281%29_A2-Net%20Generation%e2%80%99s.mht?sequence=1

Kurilovas, E., & Sėrikovienė, S. (2010). Learning content and software evaluation and personalisation problems. *Informatics in Education, An International Journal, 9*(1), 91-114. Abstract available at http://www.ceeol.com/aspx/issuedetails.aspx?issueid=d06099b8-ba56-439b-b44d-b835011d2b42&articleId=2f4d0052-9aa2-49ab-88c2-4599a7906f9a

Kurucz, P. (2006). *How to teach international students: A practical teaching guide for universities and colleges.* Nanaimo, BC: Success Orientations Publishers.

Kyei-Blankson, L., Keengwe, J., & Blankson, J. (2009). Faculty use and integration of technology in higher education. *AACE Journal, 17*(3), 199-213. Available at http://www.editlib.org/d/28362

Lafuze, J. (2012). Scavenger hunt. In R. Morgan & K. Olivares (Eds.), *Quick hits for teaching with technology: Successful strategies by award-winning teachers* (pp. 17-18). Bloomington, IN: Indiana University Press.

Lai, E. (2010). Getting in step to improve the quality of in-service teacher learning through mentoring. *Professional Development in Education, 36*(3), 443-469. doi:10.1080/19415250903115962

Lambert, J., Gong, Y., & Cuper, P. (2008). Technology, transfer and teaching: The impact of a single technology course on pre-service teachers' computer attitudes and ability. *Journal of Technology and Teacher Education, 16*(4), 385-410. Chesapeake, VA: SITE. Retrieved from http://www.editlib.org/p/26064

Lambert, L., Tice, S., & Featherstone, P. (Eds.). (1996*). University teaching: A guide for graduate students.* Syracuse, NY: Syracuse University Press.

Latham, A. (1997). Asking students the right questions. *Educational Leadership, 54*(6), 84-85.

Laverty, J., Wood, D., Tannehill, D., Kohun, F., & Turchek, J. (2012). Improving the LMS (Learning Management System) selection process: Instructor concerns, usage and perceived value of online course delivery tools. *Information Systems Education Journal, 10*(1), 75-88. Available from http://isedj.org/2012-10/N1/ISEDJv10n1p75.html

Le, A., Joordens, S., Chrysostomou, S., & Grinnell, R. (2010). Online lecture accessibility and its influence on performance in skills-based courses.

Computers & Education, 55, 313-319. Retrieved from http://www.sciencedirect.com/science/article/pii/S036013151000031X

Le, Q., & Le, M. (2012). New challenges in web-based education. In T. Le & Q. Le (Eds.), *Technologies for enhancing pedagogy, engagement and empowerment in education: Creating learning-friendly environments* (pp. 58-65). Hershey, PA: Information Science Reference.

Le, T., & Le, Q. (Eds.) (2012). *Technologies for enhancing pedagogy, engagement, and empowerment in education: Creating learning friendly environments*. Hershey, PA: Information Science reference, IGI Global.

Ledlow, S. (2001). *Using think-pair-share in the college classroom*. Phoenix, AZ: Arizona State University, Center for Learning and Teaching Excellence. Retrieved from http://www.hydroville.org/system/files/team_thinkpair-share.pdf

Lee, H, Lim, K., & Grabowski, B. (2009). Generative learning strategies and metacognitive feedback to facilitate comprehension of complex science topics and self-regulation. *Journal of Educational Multimedia and Hypermedia, 18*(1), 5-25. Chesapeake, VA: AACE. Retrieved August 2, 2013 from http://www.editlib.org/p/26119

Lehman, R., & Conceicao, S. (2013). *Retaining and motivating online students: Research-based strategies and interventions that work*. San Francisco: Jossey-Bass.

Le Maistre, C., & Pare, A. (2010). Whatever it takes: How beginning teachers learn to survive. *Teaching and Teacher Education, 26*(3), 559-564. Available at http://www.sciencedirect.com/science/article/pii/S0742051X09001449

Lepi, K. (2013a, February 1). 6 technologies that will change higher education. *Edudemic*. Retrieved from http://edudemic.com/2013/02/6-technologies-that-will-change-higher-education/

Lepi, K. (2013b, April 27). 7 ways to use your iPad in the classroom. *Edudemic*. Retrieved from http://www.edudemic.com/2013/04/7-ways-to-use-your-ipad-in-the-classroom/

Lester, S. (2009). *On professions and being professional*. Retrieved from http://www.ifl.ac.uk/__data/assets/pdf_file/0017/6803/dr-lester-professional-article-may09.pdf

Leung, K., Lue, B., & Lee, M. (2003). Development of a teaching style inventory for tutor evaluation in problem-based learning. *Medical Education, 37*(5), 410-416. Available from http://onlinelibrary.wiley.com/doi/10.1046/j.1365-2923.2003.01493.x/full

Levin, J., Nolan, J., Kerr, J., & Elliott, A. (2012). *Principles of classroom management: A professional decision-making model* (3rd Canadian ed.). Toronto, ON: Pearson

Lewis, C. (2000). Taming the lions and tigers and bears: The write [sic] way to communicate online. In K. White & B. Weight, *The online teaching guide: A handbook of attitudes, strategies, and techniques for the virtual classroom* (pp. 13-23). Boston: Allyn and Bacon.

Lieberman, A., & Friedrich, L. (2010). *How teachers become leaders.* New York: Teachers College Press.

Lightner, R. (2012). Webquests: A gateway activity for online teaching and learning. In R. Morgan, & K. Olivares (Eds.), *Quick hits for teaching with technology: Successful strategies by award-winning teachers* (Kindle Ed., pp. 81-83). Bloomington, IN: Indiana University Press.

Lindroth,T., & Bergquist, M. (2010). Laptopers in an educational practice: Promoting the personal learning situation. *Computers & Education, 54*(2), 311 -320. Retrieved from http://www.sciencedirect.com/science/article/pii/S0360131509001900

Lim, B. (1996). Students' expectations of professors. *The Teaching Professor, 10*(4), 3-4.

Lindsay, J., & Davis, V. (2013). *Flattening classrooms, engaging minds: Move to global collaboration one step at a time.* Boston, MA: Pearson.

Liu, Y. (2010), Strategies for providing formative feedback to maximize learner satisfaction and online learning. In H. Yang & S. Yuen (Eds.), *Handbook of research on practices and outcomes in e-learning: Issues and trends* (pp. 150-163). Hershey, PA: IGI Publishing.

Lockyer, J., Fidler, H., De Gara, C., & Keefe, J. (2010). Mentorship for the physician recruited from abroad to Canada for rural practice. *Medical Teacher, 32*(8), e322-e327. doi:10.3109/01421591003686237

Lombardi, J. (2008). To portfolio or not to portfolio: Helpful or hyped? *College Teaching, 56*(1), 7-13. Retrieved from http://proquest.umi.com/pqdweb?did=1442994441&Fmt=7&clientId=12306&RQT=309&VName=PQD

Lonn, S., & Teasley, S. D. (2009). Saving time or innovating practice: Investigating perceptions and uses of Learning Management Systems. *Computers & Education, 53*(3), 686-694. Available from https://ctools.umich.edu/access/content/group/research/papers/CAE1356.pdf

Lorber, M., Al-Bataineh, A., & Meyer, B. (2005). *Objectives, methods, and evaluation for secondary teaching* (5th ed.). Boston, MA: Pearson Allyn and Bacon.

Louw, J., Brown, C., Muller, J., & Soudien, C. (2009). Instructional technologies in social science instruction in South Africa. *Computers & Education, 53,* 234–242. Retrieved from http://www.sciencedirect.com/science/article/pii/S0360131509000402

Love, P., & Love, A. (1996). The interrelatedness of intellectual, social, and emotional influences on student learning. *The National Teaching & Learning Forum, 5*(5), 8-10.

Lowman, J. (1987). Giving students feedback. In M. Weimer (Ed.), *Teaching large classes well* (pp. 71-83). San Francisco: Jossey-Bass.

Lu, M., Todd, A., & Miller, M. (2011). Creating a supportive culture for online teaching: A case study of a faculty learning community. *Online Journal of Distance Learning Administration, 14*(3). Available at http://www.westga.edu/~distance/ojdla/fall143/lu_todd_miller143.html

Luyegu, E. (2012). Intercultural awareness in e-learning. In T. Le & Q. Le (Eds.), *Technologies for enhancing pedagogy, engagement and empowerment in education: Creating learning-friendly environments* (pp. 172-182). Hershey, PA: Information Science Reference.

Lynch, M., & Roecker, J. (2007). *Project managing e-learning: A handbook for successful design, delivery and management*. Abingdon, Oxon, UK: Routledge. Available at http://iplhairremovalmachines.com/book/download-Project-Managing-E-Learning-A-Handbook-for-Successful-Design-Delivery-and-Management/p1874076930/

Ma, Y., & Harmon, S.W. (2009). A case study of design-based research for creating a vision prototype of a technology-based innovative learning environment. *Journal of Interactive Learning Research, 20*(1), 75-93. Chesapeake, VA: AACE. Retrieved from http://www.editlib.org/p/25226

MacPherson, C. (2014, February 21). Provost asks can universities change? *On Campus News, 21*(12), 4. Saskatoon, Saskatchewan, Canada: University of Saskatchewan. Retrieved from http://words.usask.ca/news/files/OCN_Feb28_web.pdf

Madden, M., Lenhart, A., Cortesi, S., Gasser, U., Duggan, M., Smith, A & Beaton, M. (2013, May 21). *Teens, social media, and privacy*. Washington, DC: Pew Research Center's Internet & American Life Project, Pew Research Center (Pewinternet.org) and Berkman Center for Internet & Society at Harvard University. Available at http://pewinternet.org/Reports/2013/Teens-Social-Media-And-Privacy.aspx

Malamed, C. (2011, June 19). How to get your learners pumped: 30 ways to motivate adult learners. *ELN Insights*. Retrieved from http://insights.elearningnetwork.org/?p=40

Mandernach, B., Forrest, K., Babutzke, J., & Manker, L. (2009, March). The role of instructor interactivity in promoting critical thinking in online and face-to-face classrooms. *MERLOT Journal of Online Learning and Teaching, 5*(1). Retrieved from http://jolt.merlot.org/vol5no1/mandernach_0309.htm

Mann, S. (2011). Using findings from the performance appraisal literature to inform the evaluation of students in higher education. *Canadian Journal of*

Higher Education, 41(2), 1-9. Retrieved from http://ojs.library.ubc.ca/index.php/cjhe/article/view/2296

Manning, S., & Johnson, K. (2011). *The technology tool-belt for teaching.* San Francisco: Jossey-Bass.

Margaryan, A., Littlejohn, A., & Vojt, G. (2011). Are digital natives a myth or reality? University students' use of digital technologies. *Computers & Education, 56*(2), 429-440. Available at http://ca.yhs4.search.yahoo.com/r/_ylt=AwrTccZr3rhSzXoAb98XFwx.;_ylu=X3oDMTByMjAxbTBkBHNlYwNzcgRwb3MDNQRjb2xvA2dxMQR2dGlkAw--/SIG=13dt5gtrr/EXP=1387876075/**http%3a//www.unil.ch/webdav/site/magellan/shared/Are_digital_natives_a_myth_or_reality_.pdf

Martin, A. (2014). Motivation to learn. In A. Holliman (Ed.), *The Routledge international companion to educational psychology* (104-116). New York: Routledge.

Mate, D., Brizio, A., Tirassa, M. (2010). Effectiveness of teaching styles on learning motivation. In M. Pedrosa-de-Jesus, C. Evans, Z. Charlesworth, & E. Cools (Eds.), *Proceedings of the 15th Annual International Conference of the European Learning Styles Information Networ*k (pp. 290-298). Aveiro, Portugal, June 28-30). Retrieved from http://cogprints.org/7070/1/2010-Teaching-ELSIN.htm

Mayer, R. (2001). *Multimedia learning.* Cambridge, UK: Cambridge University Press.

McCabe, D., & Pavela, G. (2000, September/October). Some good news about academic integrity. *Change* (pp. 32-38). Retreived from http://abacus.bates.edu/cbb/events/docs/McCabe_Some.pdf

McCabe, D., & Trevino, L. (1996). What we know about cheating in college. *Change, 28*(1), 28-33.

McCarthy, J. W., Smith, J. L., & DeLuca, D. (2010). Using online discussion boards with large and small groups to enhance learning of assistive technology. *Journal of Computing in Higher Education, 22*(2), 95-113. Available at http://link.springer.com/article/10.1007%2Fs12528-010-9031-6/fulltext.html

McElmurry, K. (2012). A source for lecture launchers: Mining public media for accessible illustrations. In R. Morgan & K. Olivares (Eds.), *Quick hits for teaching with technology: Successful strategies by award-winning teachers* (pp. 22-24). Bloomington, IN: Indiana University Press.

McFerrin, K., & Christensen, P. (2013). Developing a positive asynchronous online discussion forum. *In Society for Information Technology & Teacher Education International Conference*, 2013(1), pp. 769-774. Abstract available at http://www.editlib.org/noaccess/48205

McGettigan, A. (2013, May 12). *Q. Will MOOCS be the scourge or saviour of higher education?* The Guardian, Retrieved from http://www.guardian.co.uk/commentisfree/2013/may/12/moocs-scourge-saviour-higher-education

McIntosh, P., & Warren, D. (Eds.). (2013). *Creativity in the classroom: Case studies in using the arts in teaching and learning in higher education.* Bristol, UK: Intellect Books.

McLaughlin, P. (2010). *The motivational potential of the use of information and communication technology on adult learners within adult education centres in the north west of Ireland: A case study approach* (Master's thesis). University of Limerick. Retrieved from http://ulir.ul.ie/bitstream/handle/10344/966/Patricia%20Mc%20Laughlin%20Masters%20Thesis.pdf?sequence=2

McLuhan, M., & McLuhan, E. (1992). *Laws of media: The new science.* Toronto: University of Toronto Press.

McMillan, J. (2002). Fundamental assessment principles for teachers and school administrators. In K. Cauley, F. Linder, & J. McMillan (Eds.), *Annual editions: Educational psychology 02/03* (17th ed., pp. 182-185). Guilford, CT: McGraw-Hill Dushkin.

McMillan, J., Singh, J., & Simonetta, L. (2002). The tyranny of self-oriented self-esteem. In K. Cauley, F. Linder, & J. McMillan (Eds.), *Annual editions: Educational psychology 02/03* (17th ed., pp. 103-105). Guilford, CT: McGraw-Hill Dushkin.

Medina, J. (2008). *Brain rules: 12 principles for surviving and thriving at home, work, and school.* Seattle, WA: Pear Press.

Menchaca, M., & Bekele, T. (2008). Learner and instructor identified success factors in distance education. *Distance Education, 29*(3), 231-252. Retrieved from http://search.ebscohost.com/login.aspx?direct=true&db=a9h&AN=34506521&loginpage=Login.asp&site=ehost-live

Mentkowski, M., & Associates. (2000). *Learning that lasts: Integrating learning, development, and performance on college and beyond.* San Francisco, CA: Jossey-Bass.

Merriam, S., Caffarella, R., & Baumgartner, L. (2007). *Learning in adulthood: A comprehensive guide* (3rd ed.). San Francisco: Jossey-Bass.

Meyer, J., Land, R., & Baillie, C. (Eds.). (2010). *Threshold concepts and transformational learning.* Rotterdam, The Netherlands: Sense Publishers.

Mezirow, J. 1991. *Transformative dimensions of adult learning.* San Francisco: Jossey Bass.

Micarelli, A., Sciarrone, F., & Gasparetti, F. (2011). A case-based approach to adaptive hypermedia navigation. In E. Ng., N. Karacapilidis, & M. Raisinghani (Eds.), *Dynamic advancements in teaching and learning based technologies: New concepts* (pp. 46-65). Hershey, PA: Information Science Reference.

Miller, M. (2012). *From denial to acceptance: The stages of assessment.* Champaign, IL: National Institute for Learning Outcomes Assessment. Retrieved from http://www.learningoutcomeassessment.org/documents/Miller.pdf

Minocha, S., & Roberts, D. (2011). Social, usability and pedagogical factors influencing students' learning experiences with wikis and blogs. In I. Dror (Ed.), *Technology enhanced learning and cognition (pp.* 97–131). Amsterdam, The Netherlands: John Benjamins.

Mishra, P., & Koehler, M. (2006). Technological pedagogical content knowledge: A framework for teacher knowledge. *Teachers College Record, 108*(6), 1017–1054. Retrieved from http://punya.educ.msu.edu/publications/journal_articles/mishra-koehler-tcr2006.pdf

Moore, Holly. (2014, February 26). Campus cheaters hire custom essay writers to avoid detection [Online news article, Canadian Broadcasting Corporation News]. Retrieved from http://www.cbc.ca/news/canada/manitoba/campus-cheaters-hire-custom-essay-writers-to-avoid-detection-1.2551409

Moreno, R. (2012). Application of technology to learning. In K. Harris, S. Graham, & T. Urban (Eds.), *APA educational psychology handbook, Volume 3: Application of technology to learning* (pp. 427-449). Washington, DC: American Psychological Association.

Morgan, R. (2012). Assessment: An opportunity to demonstrate excellence. In R. Morgan & K. Olivares (Eds.), *Quick hits for teaching with technology: Successful strategies by award-winning teachers* (p. 63). Bloomington, IN: Indiana University Press.

Morrone, M. (2012). Blogging to promote robust class preparation. In R. Morgan & K. Olivares (Eds.), *Quick hits for teaching with technology: Successful strategies by award-winning teachers* (pp. 96-97). Bloomington, IN: Indiana University Press.

Morse, J. (1995). A yes for group work. *The Teaching Professor, 9*(9), 3-4.

Mosteller, F. (1989). The "muddiest point in the lecture" as a feedback device. *On Teaching and Learning: The Journal of the Harvard-Danforth Center, 3*, 10-21.

Mouzakis, C. (2008). Teachers' perceptions of the effectiveness of a blended learning approach for ICT teacher training. *Journal of Technology and Teacher Education, 16*(4), 461-482. Chesapeake, VA: SITE. Retrieved from http://www.editlib.org/p/24384.

Mukherjee, M. (2012). Evaluating educational software: A historical overview and the challenges ahead. In T. Le & Q. Le (Eds.), *Technologies for en-*

hancing pedagogy, engagement and empowerment in education: Creating learning-friendly environments (pp. 264-276). Hershey, PA: Information Science Reference.

Murphy, E., & Ángeles Rodríguez-Manzanares, M. (2008). Revisiting transactional distance theory in a context of web-based high-school distance education. *Journal Of Distance Education, 22*(2), 1-14. Retrieved from http://www.jofde.ca/index.php/jde/article/view/38/549

Murphy, P. (Ed.). (1999). *Learners, learning & assessment.* Thousand Oaks, CA: Sage.

Murray, C. (2011). Imagine mobile learning in your pocket. In W. Ng (Ed.), *Mobile technologies and handheld devices for ubiquitous learning: Research and pedagogy* (pp. 209-236). Hershey, PA: Information Science Reference.

Murray, H. (1987). Acquiring student feedback that improves instruction. In M. Weimer (Ed.), *Teaching large classes well* (pp. 85-96). San Francisco: Jossey-Bass.

Nadelstern, E. (2013). *10 lessons from New York City schools: What really works to improve education.* New York: Teachers College Press.

Nandi, D., Hamilton, M., & Harland, J. (2012). Evaluating the quality of interaction in asynchronous discussion forums in fully online courses. *Distance Education, 33*(1), 5-30. Available at http://ca.yhs4.search.yahoo.com/r/_ylt=AwrTccG6rLlSjFMAk8kXFwx.;_ylu=X3oDMTBya DNhc2JxBHNlYwNzcgRwb3MDMQRjb2xvA2dxMQR2dGlkAw--/SIG=12hpj7olr/EXP=1387928890/**http%3a//researchbank.rmit.edu.au/eserv/rmit%3a160364/Nandi.pdf

New Media Consortium. (2013). *NMC horizon report 2014: Higher education preview.* Austin, Texas: Author. Retrieved from http://www.nmc.org/pdf/2014-horizon-he-preview.pdf

Ng, E., Karacapilidis, N., & Raisinghani, M. (Eds). (2011). *Dynamic advancements in teaching and learning based technologies: New concepts.* Hershey PA: Information Science Reference

Ng, L., Hewitt, L., Turton, E., McLennan, R., & Davey, P. (2011). Practical examination grading via paper and iPads. In J. Yorke (Ed.), *Meeting the challenges. Proceedings of the ATN (Australian Technology Network) Assessment Conference,* 20-21 October (p. 39). Perth, Western Australia: Curtin University. Retrieved from http://otl.curtin.edu.au/professional_development/conferences/atna2011/files/ATNA_2011_Proceedings.pdf

Ng, W., & Anastopoulou, S. (2011). Formal and informal use of handhelds by Australian and British students. In W. Ng (Ed.), *Mobile technologies and handheld devices for ubiquitous learning: Research and pedagogy* (pp. 279-298). Hershey, PA: Information Science Reference.

Nicholas, H. (2011). Ubiquitous computing does not guarantee ubiquitous learning in schools: The case of handheld computers. In W. Ng (Ed.), *Mobile technologies and handheld devices for ubiquitous learning: Research and pedagogy* (pp. 30-44). Hershey, PA: Information Science Reference.

Niedzlek-Feaver, M., & Black, B. (2012). Sometimes less is more. In R. Morgan, & K. Olivares (Eds.), *Quick hits for teaching with technology: Successful strategies by award-winning teachers* (Kindle Ed., pp. 68-69). Bloomington, IN: Indiana University Press.

Nihalani, M., & Shah, S. (2012). *Stress free environment in classroom: Impact of humor in student satisfaction.* Munich, Germany: Grin Verlag Publisher.

Nilson, L. (2010). *Teaching at its best: A research-based resource for College instructors* (3rd ed.). Hoboken, NJ: Anker Publishing Jossey-Bass Wiley.

Nord, W. (1990). Teaching and morality: The knowledge most worth having. In D. Dill and associates (Eds.), *What teachers need to know: The knowledge, skills, and values essential to good teaching* (pp. 173-198). San Francisco: Jossey-Bass.

Nothing succeeds like success. (1994, October). *University Affairs, 35*(8), 28.

Notterman, J., & Drewry, H. (1993). *Psychology and education: Parallel and interactive approaches.* New York: Plenum.

Novak, G. (2012). Technology transforming learning. In R. Morgan, & K. Olivares (Eds.), *Quick hits for teaching with technology: Successful strategies by award-winning teachers* (pp. 1-3). Bloomington, IN: Indiana University Press.

Nunn, C. (1996). Discussion details. *The Teaching Professor, 10*(7), 5.

OER (Open Educational Resources) Africa. (n.d.). *Using technology in African higher education.* Author, South African Institute for Distance Education (SAIDE). Retrieved from http://www.oerafrica.org/technology/TechnologyTrends/tabid/1332/Default.aspx

Ogrenci, A. S. (2012, June). Empirical results about efforts for effective teaching to y-generation freshman students. In *Information Technology Based Higher Education and Training* (ITHET), 2012 International Conference (pp. 1-5), IEEE. Available at http://ieeexplore.ieee.org/xpls/abs_all.jsp?arnumber=6246043&tag=1

O'Hara, S., & Pritchard, R. (2012). "I'm teaching what?!": Preparing university faculty for online instruction. *Journal of Educational Research and Practice, 2*(1). Available at http://ca.yhs4.search.yahoo.com/r/_ylt=AwrTccInurlSnEkAd_kXFwx.;_ylu=X3oDMTByaDNhc2JxBHNlYwNzcgRwb3MDMQRjb2xvA2dxMQR2dGlkAw--/SIG=138vm3dol/EXP=1387932327/**http%3a//www.publishing.waldenu.edu/cgi/viewcontent.cgi%3farticle=1032%26context=jerap

Oliva, P., & Gordon, W. II. (2013). *Developing the curriculum* (8th ed.). Toronto: Pearson.

Oliveira, I., Tinoca, L., & Pereira, A. (2011). Online group work patterns: How to promote a successful collaboration, *Computers and Education, 57*(1). Retrieved from http://www.sciencedirect.com/science/article/pii/S0360131511000340

Organization for Economic Co-operation and Development. (2003). *Beyond rhetoric: Adult learning policies and practices.* Paris, France: OECD.

Orlich, D., Harder, R., Callahan, R., Trevisan, M., Brown, A., & Miller, D. (2013). *Teaching strategies: A guide to effective instruction* (10th ed.). Belmont, CA: Wadsworth Cengage.

Osborne, R., & Kriese, P.(2012). Promoting engagement in an online course: It can be done, but wisely! In R. Morgan & K. Olivares (Eds.), *Quick hits for teaching with technology: Successful strategies by award-winning teachers* (Kindle Ed., pp. 5-6). Bloominton, IN: Indiana University Press.

Owens, J. (2012). YouTube reviews. In R. Morgan, & K. Olivares (Eds.), *Quick hits for teaching with technology: Successful strategies by award-winning teachers* (Kindle Ed., pp. 8-10). Bloominton, IN: Indiana University Press.

Owston, R. (2013). Blended learning policy and implementation: Introduction to the special issue. *The Internet and Higher Education, 18,* 1–3. doi.org/10.1016/j.iheduc.2013.03.002 Retrieved from http://www.sciencedirect.com/science/article/pii/S1096751613000134

Oztok, M., Zingaro, D., Brett, C., & Hewitt, J. (2013). Exploring asynchronous and synchronous tool use in online courses, *Computers & Education, 60*(1), 87-94. Available at http://www.sciencedirect.com/science/article/pii/S0360131512001935

Pace, D. (2012). Prezi and the decoding of history. In R. Morgan & K. Olivares (Eds.), *Quick hits for teaching with technology: Successful strategies by award-winning teachers* (p. 90-92). Bloomington, IN: Indiana University Press

Palloff, R., & Pratt, K. (2013*). Lessons from the virtual classroom: The realities of online teaching* (2nd ed.). San Francisco: Jossey-Bass.

Palmer, P. (2010). *The courage to teach: Exploring the inner landscape of a teacher's life* (2nd ed.). San Francisco, CA: Wiley.

Pappas, C. (2013a, April 26). 17 tips to motivate adult learners. *eLearning Industry.* Retrieved from http://elearningindustry.com/17-tips-to-motivate-adult-learners

Pappas, C. (2013b, May 8). 8 important characteristics of adult learners. *eLearning Industry.* Retrieved from http://elearningindustry.com/8-important-characteristics-of-adult-learners

Pappas, C. (2013c, June 1). 69 free adobe flash cs6 video tutorials. *eLearning Industry*. Retrieved from http://elearningindustry.com/69-free-adobe-flash-cs6-video-tutorials

Pappas, C. (2013d, December 1*)*. Top 10 e-learning statistics for 2014 you need to know. *eLearning Industry*. Retrieved from http://elearningindustry.com/top-10-e-learning-statistics-for-2014-you-need-to-know

Parkay, F., Hardcastle Stanford, B., Vaillancourt, J., Stephens, H., & Harris, J. (2012). *Becoming a teacher* (4th Canadian ed.). Toronto, ON: Pearson Canada

Parkay, F., Anctil, E., & Hass, G. (Eds.). (2014). *Curriculum leadership: Readings for developing quality educational programs*. New York: Pearson.

Parker, K., Lenhart, A., & Moore, K. (2011, August 28). *The digital revolution and higher education social and demographic trends* (Education Report). Pew Research Center. Retrieved from http://www.pewinternet.org/Reports/2011/College-presidents.aspx

Parr, C. (2013, May 17). Embrace MOOCS or face decline, warns v-c. *Times Higher Education*. Retrieved from http://www.timeshighereducation.co.uk/news/embrace-moocs-or-face-decline-warns-v-c/2003919.article

Paul, R. (1987). Dialogical thinking: Critical thought essential to the acquisition of rational knowledge and passions. In J. Baron & R. Sternberg (Eds*.)*, *Teaching thinking skills: Theory and practice* (pp. 127-148). New York: Freeman.

Perrone, V. (1991). Introduction. In V. Perrone (Ed.), *Expanding student assessment* (pp. vii-xi). Alexandria, VA: Association for Supervision and Curriculum Development.

Phillips, M. (2003). Delivering learner support on-line. In A. Tait & R. Mills (Eds.), *Rethinking learner support in distance education: Change and continuity in an international context* (168 –183). Abingdon, UK: Routledge.

Piscioneri, M. (2012). Is all that glitters gold? Re-thinking e-learning and education revolutions. In T. Le & Q. Le (Eds.), *Technologies for enhancing pedagogy, engagement and empowerment in education: Creating learning-friendly environments* (pp. 287-299). Hershey, PA: Information Science Reference.

Pollio, H., & Humphreys, W. (1988). Grading students. In J. McMillan (Ed.), *Assessing students' learning* (pp. 85-97). San Francisco: Jossey-Bass.

Prensky, M. (2010). *Teaching digital natives: Partnering for real learning*. Thousand Oaks, CA: Corwin.

Prince, M. (2004). Does active learning work? A review of the research. *Journal of Engineering Education, 93,* 223-231.

Proulx, C. (2012). *5 ways technology will impact higher ed in 2013.* Retrieved from http://www.forbes.com/sites/groupthink/2012/12/11/5-ways-technology-will-impact-higher-ed-in-2013/

Purcell, K., Buchanan, J., & Friedrich, L. (2013, July 16). The impact of digital tools on student writing and how writing is taught in schools. Report from the PEW Research Center (Summary). Retrieved from http://www.pewinternet.org/Reports/2013/Teachers-technology-and-writing.aspx

Purdue University. (2012). *ASBMB-RCN workshop: Assessment of students' reasoning with core concepts and visualizations in biochemistry.* Retrieved from http://www.asbmb.org/uploadedFiles/NSF/Meetings/2011-2012_Regional_Meetings/AssessmentAll.pdf

Raffini, J. (1993). *Winners without losers.* Boston: Allyn and Bacon.

Rakes, G., & Dunn, K. (2010). The impact of online graduate students' motivation and self- regulation on academic procrastination. *Journal of Interactive Online Learning, 9*(1), 78-93.

Ralph, E. (1982). The unmotivated second-language learner: Can students' negative attitudes be changed? *The Canadian Modern Language Review, 38*(3), 493-502.

Ralph, E. (1989). Research on effective teaching: How can it help L2 teachers motivate the unmotivated learner? *The Canadian Modern Language Review, 46*(1), 135-146.

Ralph, E. (1994). Beginning teachers as effective classroom managers: How are they?...Managing? *McGill Journal of Education, 29*(2), 181-196.

Ralph, E. (1995a). The transfer of knowledge from practicum to practice: Novice teachers' views. *Brock University, 5*(1), 6-21.

Ralph, E. (1995b). Toward instructional improvement: Reflections and insights on a Canadian journey. *The Journal of Graduate Teaching Assistant Development, 2*(3), 125-133.

Ralph, E. (1996). Improving teaching through cross-college collaboration: Reflections on a Saskatchewan experience. *McGill Journal of Education, 31,* 297-318.

Ralph, E. (1997a). Teaching to the test: Principles of authentic assessment for second language education. In A. Mollica (Ed.), *Teaching languages* (pp. 249-257). Welland, ON: Soleil.

Ralph, E. (1997b). The power of dramatics in teaching: Reflections on some recollections. *McGill Journal of Education, 32*(3), 273-288. Retrieved from http://mje.mcgill.ca/article/view/8382/6310

Ralph, E. (1998). *Motivating teaching in higher education: A manual for faculty development.* Stillwater, OK: New Forums Press.

Ralph, E. (1999). Developing novice teachers' oral-questioning skills. *McGill Journal of Education, 34*(1), 29-47. Retrieved from http://www.google.ca/url?sa=t&rct=j&q=&esrc=s&frm=1&source=web&cd=2&ved=0CCwQFjAB&url=http%3A%2F%2Fmje.mcgill.ca%2Farticle%2Fdownload%2F4653%2F6388&ei=dXwaU8S-AcjfoAT0rILgDQ&usg=AFQjCNHUVwtlo5cIirBPra2qAPV_w1suhA

Ralph, E. (2004). *Pursuing instructional effectiveness in higher eduation: It's about time!* New York: Nova Science.

Ralph. E. (Ed.). (2005). *College teaching.* New York: Novalinka.

Ralph, E., & Konchak, P. (1996). Implications for improving teaching in the health sciences: Some Canadian findings. *Quality in Higher Education, 2*(1), 45-55.

Ralph, E., & Noonan, B. (2004). Evaluating teacher-candidates' teaching in the extended practicum. *Brock Education, 14* (1), 1-18.

Ralph, E., & Walker, K. (Eds.). (2011). *Adapting mentorship across the professions: Fresh insights and perspectives* Calgary, Alberta, Canada: Temeron/Detselig.

Ralph, E., & Walker, K. (2012). Enhancing mentoring across the disciplines: Via the Adaptive Mentorship model. *Bridges: Reflecting the scholarship of teaching & learning at the University of Saskatchewan, 10*(3), 9-11.

Ralph, E., & Walker, K. (2013). The efficacy of the Adaptive Mentorship model. *Open Journal of Leadership, 2*(2), 1-6. Available online from http://www.scirp.org/journal/PaperInformation.aspx?PaperID=32622

Ralph, E., & Yang, B. (1993). Beginning teachers' utilization of instructional media: A Canadian case study. *Educational & Training Technology International, 30*(4), 299-318.

Ramsden, P. (2003). *Learning to teach in higher education* (2nd ed.). New York: Routledge Falmer.

Ramsden, P. (2011, March 10). *Six principles of effective teaching in higher education.* Retrieved from http://paulramsden48.wordpress.com/category/principles-of-good-teaching/

Reeves, D. (2011). *Finding your leadership focus: What matters most for student results.* New York: Teachers College Press.

Reeves, T.C. (2009). *Little learning, big learning: In defense of authentic tasks.* Presented at World Conference on Educational Multimedia, Hypermedia and Telecommunications 2009. Retrieved August 3, 2013 from http://www.editlib.org/p/31454

Reich, J., & Daccord, T. (2008). *Best ideas for teaching with technology: A practical guide for teachers, by teachers.* Armonk, NY: M.E. Sharpe.

Reid, P. (2012). Categories for barriers to adoption of instructional technologies. *Education and Information Technologies*. Available at http://link.springer.com/article/10.1007%2Fs10639-012-9222-z/fulltext.html

Reigeluth, C. (1996). Instructional design: Guidelines and theories. In A. Tuijnman (Ed.), *International encyclopedia of adult education and training* (2nd ed., pp. 497-503). New York: Elsevier Science.

Reio, T. Jr., & Wiswell, A. (2000). Field investigation of the relationship among adult curiosity, workplace learning, and job performance. *Human Resource Development Quarterly, 11*(1), 5–30. doi: 10.1002/1532-1096(200021)11:1<5::AID-HRDQ2>3.0.CO;2-A Retrieved from http://onlinelibrary.wiley.com/doi/10.1002/1532-1096%28200021%2911:1%3C5::AID-HRDQ2%3E3.0.CO;2-A/full

Reyes, K. (2013a, March). Learning, creativity, and fun with pictures. *Outreach and Technical Assistance Network for Adult Educators*. Retrieved from http://www.otan.us/browse/index.cfm?fuseaction=view_ft&catid=33921&recno=4989

Reyes, K. (2013b, May). Socrative: A byod audience response system for formative assessment. *Outreach and Technical Assistance Network for Adult Educators*. Retrieved from http://www.otan.us/browse/index.cfm?fuseaction=browse&catid=10722

Rivard, R. (2013, May 14). Massive (but not open). *Inside Higher Ed.* Retrieved from http://www.insidehighered.com/news/2013/05/14/georgia-tech-and-udacity-roll-out-massive-new-low-cost-degree-program

Roberts, R. (2010). The digital generation and Web 2.0: E-learning concern or media myth? In H. Yang & S. Yuen (Eds.), *Handbook of research on practices and outcomes in e-learning: Issues and trends* (pp. 93-115). Hershey, PA: IGI Publishing.

Robinson, D., & Schraw, G. (2008). *Recent innovations in educational technology that facilitate student learning*. Charlotte, NC: Information Age.

Roesky, H., & Kennepohl, D. (2008). Drawing attention with chemistry cartoons. *Journal of Chemical Education, 85*(10), 1355-1360. Retrieved from http://search.ebscohost.com/login.aspx?direct=true&db=a9h&AN=34461488&loginpage=Login.asp&site=ehost-live

Rohrbacher, C. (2012). Using personal response devices (clickers) in humanities classes. In R. Morgan & K. Olivares (Eds.), *Quick hits for teaching with technology: Successful strategies by award-winning teachers* (p. 74-75). Bloomington, IN: Indiana University Press.

Rolf, D. (2012). Mixed realities: Human interaction technologies. In T. Le & Q. Le (Eds.), *Technologies for enhancing pedagogy, engagement and empowerment in education: Creating learning-friendly environments* (pp. 209-216). Hershey, PA: Information Science Reference.

Rubie-Davies, C. (2011). *Educational psychology: Concepts, research and challenges.* New York: Routledge.

Rubin, B., Fernandes, R., Avgerinou, M., & Moore, J. (2010). The effect of learning management systems on student and faculty outcomes. *The Internet and Higher Education, 13*(1), 82-83. Available at http://www.sciencedirect.com/science/article/pii/S1096751609000657#

Rueda, R. (2011). *The 3 dimensions of improving student performance.* New York: Teachers College Press. [Learning, Motivational; Organizational. Tasks equipment must be relevant useful and meaningful]

Ruru, D., Sanga, K., Walker, K., & Ralph, E. (2013). Adapting mentorship across the professions: A Fijian view. *International Journal of Evidence Based Coaching and Mentoring, 11*(2), 70-93. Retrieved from http://ijebcm.brookes.ac.uk/documents/vol11issue2-paper-06.pdf

Ryan, J. (2013).Motivation in adult learning. *Slideshare, Inc.* Retrieved from http://www.slideshare.net/coachjoeryan/motivation-in-adult-learning

Ryan, R., & Deci, E. (2002). Intrinsic and extrinsic motivations: Classic definitions and new directions. In K. Cauley, F. Linder, & J. McMillan (Eds.), *Annual editions: Educational psychology 02/03* (17th ed., pp. 132-138). Guilford, CT: McGraw-Hill Dushkin.

Sadasivam, R., Crenshaw, K., Schoen, M., & Datla, R. (2010). Transforming continuing healthcare education with e-learning 2.0. In H. Yang & S. Yuen (Eds.), *Handbook of research on practices and outcomes in e-learning: Issues and trends* (pp. 308-327). Hershey, PA: IGI Publishing.

Salmon, G., & Edirisingha, P. (2008). *Podcasting for learning in universities.* New York: Open University Press.

Saskatchewan Professional Development Unit. (1994, Fall). Lecturing myths. *Instructional Strategies Series Newsletter, 3*(3), 2-3. Saskatoon, SK: Author.

Saxena Arora, A., & Raisinghani, M. (2011). Redefining web users' optimal flow experiences in online environments: An empirical analysis. In E. Ng., N. Karacapilidis, & M. Raisinghani (Eds.), *Dynamic advancements in teaching and learning based technologies: New concepts* (pp. 181-195). Hershey, PA: Information Science Reference.

Schifter, C. (Ed.). (2008*). Infusing technology into the classroom: Continuous practice improvement.* Hershey, PA: Information Science Publishing.

Schon, D. (1995). The new scholarship requires a new epistemology: Knowing in action. *Change, 27*(6), 26-34.

Schor Ko, S, & Rossen, S. (2008). *Teaching online: A practical guide* (2nd ed.). New York: Routledge.

Schultz, R. (2012). Enhancing teaching and learning through technology. In R. Morgan & K. Olivares (Eds.), *Quick hits for teaching with technology: Suc-*

cessful strategies by award-winning teachers (p. 72-73). Bloomington, IN: Indiana University Press.

Scott, C., & Schwartz, J. (2012). Using a business strategy simulation. In R. Morgan & K. Olivares (Eds.), *Quick hits for teaching with technology: Successful strategies by award-winning teachers* (p. 28). Bloomington, IN: Indiana University Press.

Sergiovanni, T. (1992). *Moral leadership: Getting to the heart of school improvement.* San Francisco, CA: Jossey-Bass.

Shannon-Karasik, C. (2013, March 15). Exciting education game-changers in 2013. *Campus Explorer, Inc.* Retrieved from http://www.campusexplorer.com/college-advice-tips/8FD9DA46/Exciting-Education-Game-Changers-in-2013/

Shell, D., & Warner, B. (2012). Some assembly required: Teaching online with good instructions. In R. Morgan & K. Olivares (Eds.), *Quick hits for teaching with technology: Successful strategies by award-winning teachers* (pp. 38-39). Blominton, IN: Indiana University Press.

Shi, Y., Fan, S., & Yue, Y. (2012). Empowering students in computer-supported education. In T. Le & Q. Le (Eds.), *Technologies for enhancing pedagogy, engagement and empowerment in education: Creating learning-friendly environments* (pp. 198-207). Hershey, PA: Information Science Reference.

Shils, E. (1983). *The academic ethic* (The report of a study group of the International Council on the Future of the University). Chicago, IL: University of Chicago Press.

Shin, T., Koehler, M., Mishra, P., Schmidt, D., Baran, E., & Thompson, A. (2009). Changing technological pedagogical content knowledge (TPACK) through course experiences. In I. Gibson et al. (Eds.), *Proceedings of Society for Information Technology & Teacher Education International Conference, 2009* (pp. 4152-4159). Chesapeake, VA: AACE. Retrieved from http://www.editlib.org/p/31309.

Showers, B., Joyce, B., & Bennett, B. (1987). Synthesis of research on staff development: A framework for future study and a state-of-the-art analysis. *Educational Leadership, 45*(3), 77-87.

Shulman, L. (1987). Knowledge and teaching: Foundations of the new reform. *Harvard Educational Review, 57*, 1-22.

Shulman, L. (1993). Teaching as community property: Putting an end to pedagogical solitude. *Change, 25*(6), 6-7.

Simon, J. (2012). Promoting online courses' student engagement and group cohesion through the use of chat-rooms. In R. Morgan, & K. Olivares (Eds.), *Quick hits for teaching with technology: Successful strategies by award-winning teachers* (Kindle Ed., pp.10-11). Bloomington, IN: Indiana University Press.

Sims, S., & Sims, R. (1995a). Learning and learning styles: A review and look to the future. In R. Sims & S. Sims (Eds.), *The importance of learning styles* (pp. 193-210). Westport, CT: Greenwood.

Sims, R., & Sims, S. (1995b). Learning enhancement in higher education. In R. Sims & S. Sims (Eds.), *The importance of learning styles* (pp. 1-24). Westport, CT: Greenwood.

Skelton, A. (2007). *International perspectives on teaching excellence in higher education : Improving knowledge and practice.* New York: Routledge.

Skrabut, S. (2013). *How teaching adults impacts your instruction.* Slideshare, Inc. Retrieved from http://www.slideshare.net/skrabut/how-teaching-adults-impacts-your-instruction?from_search=20

Slavin, R. (2011). *Educational psychology: Theory and practice* (10th ed.). Boston, MA: Pearson Allyn and Bacon.

Smith, C. (2008). Building effectiveness in teaching through targeted evaluation and response: Connecting evaluation to teaching improvement in higher education. *Assessment & Evaluation in Higher Education, 33*(5), 517-533. Available from http://www.tandfonline.com/doi/full/10.1080/02602930701698942#.UrnL-fuPU68

Smith, K. (Ed.). (2007). *Teaching, learning, assessing: A guide for effective teaching at college and university.* Oakville, ON : Mosaic Press.

Smith, K., Bichelmeyer, B., Monson, J., & Horvitz, B. (2007). Integrating computers in the schools: A review of criticisms. In M. Orey, V. McClendon, & R. Branch (Eds.), *Educational Media and Technology Yearbook 2007* (pp. 3-19). Littleton, CO: Libraries Unlimited, Inc.

Smith, T. C. (2005). Fifty-one competencies for online instruction. *The Journal of Educators Online, 2*(2), 1-18. Available from http://home.surewest.net/tcsmith/papers/index.htm

Smythe, S. (2012, May27). *Incorporating digital technologies in adult basic education: concepts, practices and recommendations.* A report for AlphaPlus. Retrieved from http://incorporatingtechnologies.alphaplus.ca/

Smyth, E., & Volker, J. (Eds.). (2013). *Enhancing instruction with visual media: Utilizing video and audio capture.* Hersey, PA: Information Science Reference.

Snowman, J., McCown, R., & Biehler, R. (2012). *Psychology applied to teaching* (13th ed.). Belmont, CA: Wadsworth

Solvie, P., & Sungur, E. (2012). Teaching for success: Technology and learning styles in preservice teacher education. *Contemporary Issues in Technology and Teacher Education, 12*(1), 6-40. Available at http://www.editlib.org/p/35444

Soto-Rojas, A. (2012). Service-learning at the seal Indiana mobile program. In R. Morgan, & K. Olivares (Eds.), *Quick hits for teaching with technology: Successful strategies by award-winning teachers* (Kindle Ed., pp.43-46). Bloomington, IN: Indiana University Press.

Soto-Rojas A., & Martinez-Mier, E. (2012). *Podcast technology self-directed lecturing for fluoride toxicity.*

Spies, M. (2011). Engaging the online learner: Student reactions to the use of audio podcasts in off campus courses. In G. Williams, P. Statham, N. Brown, & B. Cleland (Eds.), *Changing demands, changing directions: Proceedings ascilite 2011 Hobart* (pp.1167-1177). Retrieved from http://www.ascilite.org.au/conferences/hobart11/procs/Spies-full.pdf

Spitzer, B. (2012). Using podcasts for added instructional effectiveness. In R. Morgan, & K. Olivares (Eds.), *Quick hits for teaching with technology: Successful strategies by award-winning teachers* (Kindle Ed., p. 100). Bloomington, IN: Indiana University Press

Stein, D., &. Wanstreet, C. (2012). Chats: A mess or a must? In R. Morgan, & K. Olivares (Eds.), *Quick hits for teaching with technology: Successful strategies by award-winning teachers* (Kindle Ed., pp.93-94). Bloomington, IN: Indiana University Press

Stern, L. (2006). *What every student should know about avoiding plagiarism.* New York: Longman Pearson.

Sternberg, R. (1987). Questions and answers about the nature and teaching of thinking skills. In J. Baron & R. Sternberg (Eds.), *Teaching thinking skills: Theory and practice* (pp. 251-259). New York: Freeman.

Sternberg, R. (1994). Triarchic theory of human intelligence. In R. Sternberg (Ed.), *Encyclopedia of human intelligence: Vol. 2* (pp. 1087-1091). New York: Macmill

Sternberg, R. (1997). What does it mean to be smart? *Educational Leadership, 54*(6), 20-24.

Sternberg, R., & Williams, W. (2010). *Educational psychology* (2nd ed.). New York: Pearson.

Stevens, D., & Kithchenham, A. (2011). An analysis of mobile learning in education, business, and medicine. In A. Kitchenham (Ed.), *Models for interdisciplinary mobile learning: Delivering information to students* (pp. 1-25). Hershey, PA: Information Science Reference.

Stewart, D. (1993). Teaching or facilitating: A false dichotomy. *Canadian Journal of Education, 18*(1), 1-13.

Stewart, D. (1994). Teaching undiminished: A reply to my critics. *Canadian Journal of Education, 19*(3), 299-304.

Stewart, K., & Hedberg, J. (2011). The pedagogy of mobility. In W. Ng (Ed.), *Mobile technologies and handheld devices for ubiquitous learning: Research and pedagogy* (pp. 259-278). Hershey, PA: Information Science Reference.

Stice, J. (Ed.). (1987). *Developing critical thinking and problem-solving abilities.* San Francisco: Jossey-Bass.

Stipek, D. (2002). *Motivation to learn: Integrating theory and practice* (4th ed.). Boston: Pearson Allyn & Bacon.

Stödberg, U. (2012). A research review of e-assessment. *Assessment & Evaluation in Higher Education, 37*(5), 591-604. Available from http://www.tandfonline.com/doi/full/10.1080/02602938.2011.557496#.UrnPLPuPU68

Stronge, J. (2007). *Qualities of effective teachers* (2nd ed.). Alexandria, VA: Association for Supervision and Curriculum Development.

Styer, A. (2009). Motivating the adult learner online. *ICI-Global.com* (pp. 1456-1460). Retrieved from http://www.igi-global.com/viewtitlesample.aspx?id=11936

Sulla, N. (2012). *Teaching the digital generation.* [Web log post]. Retrieved from

http://www.educationworld.com/a_curr/teaching-digital-generation.shtml

Svinicki, M. (1992). Assertiveness and the college instructor. In K. Lewis (Ed.), *Teaching pedagogy to teaching assistants: A handbook for 398T instructors* (3rd ed., pp. 64-70). Austin, TX: University of Texas at Austin, Center for Teaching Effectiveness.

Swan, K., Shen, J., & Hiltz, S. R. (2006). Assessment and collaboration in online learning. *Journal of Asynchronous Learning Networks, 10*(1), 45-62. Available from http://www.acousticslab.org/dots_sample/module4/module04_additional.html

Symtext. (2010). *The new learning: Digital technologies and post-secondary education: A*

Symtext white paper. Retrieved from http://www.symtext.com/wp-content/uploads/2010/03/DIGITAL-TECHNOLOGIES-POST-SECONDARY-EDUCATION.pdf

Tamblyn, D. (2006). *Laugh and learn: 95 ways to use humor for more effective teaching and training.* New York: AMACOM (American Management Association).

Tan, Yee-Ming. (2008, November 23). Cultivating curiosity: A personal experiment.

Positive Psychology News Daily. Retrieved from http://positivepsychologynews.com/news/yee-ming-tan/200811231206

Tang, T., & Austin, M. (2009). Students' perceptions of teaching technologies, application of technologies, and academic performance. *Computers &*

Education, 53, 1241-1255. Retrieved from http://www.sciencedirect.com/science/article/pii/S0360131509001547

Tapscott, D. (2002). Educating the Net generation. In K. Cauley, F. Linder, & J. McMillan (Eds.), *Annual editions: Educational psychology 02/03* (17th ed., pp.126-129). Guilford, CT: McGraw-Hill Dushkin.

TeachThought [*sic*] Staff. (2012, August 26). *60 ways to use twitter in the classroom by category.* Retrieved from http://www.teachthought.com/social-media/60-ways-to-use-twitter-in-the-classroom-by-category/

Teo, T. (2009). Modelling technology acceptance in education: A study of pre-service teachers. *Computers & Education, 52 ,*302–312. Retrieved from http://www.sciencedirect.com/science/article/pii/S0360131508001358

The landscape: Where's the beef? College seniors evaluate their undergraduate experience. (1994). *Change, 26*(5), 29-32.

The surge of contract cheating among students. (2013, April 29). *The Higher Education 2013.* Retrieved from http://www.lsbu-multimedia-journalists.co.uk/weke/2013/04/29/another-test-2/

Thirty years of cheating. (1996, April). *The Teaching Professor, 10*(4), 6.

Tien, F., & Fu, T. (2008). The correlates of the digital divide and their impact on college student learning. *Computers & Education, 5,* 421–436. Retrieved from

http://www.sciencedirect.com/science/article/pii/S036013150600114X

Tierney, E. (1999). *101 ways to better presentations.* London, UK: Kogan Page..

Tomaszewski, J. (2012a). *Ed tech trends for 2012: Part 1.* Retrieved from http://www.educationworld.com/a_tech/tech-trends-for-2012-part-1.shtml

Tomaszewski, J. (2012b). *Ed tech trends for 2012: Part 2.* Retrieved from http://www.educationworld.com/a_tech/tech-trends-for-2012-part-2.shtml

Tomlinson, C., & McTighe, J. (2006). *Integrrating differentiated instruction and understanding by design.* Alexandria, VA: ASCD (Association for Supervision and Curriculum Development).

Torrance, E., & Myers, R. (1973). *Creative learning & teaching.* New York: Dodd, Mead.

Truebridge, S. (2014). *Resilience begins with beliefs: Building on student strengths for success in school.* New York: Teachers College Press.

Tsai, C., & Chai, C. (2012). The "third"-order barrier for technology-integration instruction: Implications for teacher education. Building the ICT capacity of the next generation of teachers in Asia. *Australasian Journal of Educational Technology, 28*(6), 1057-1060. Available from http://www.ascilite.org.au/ajet/ajet28/tsai-cc.html

Tsai, M., Liang, J., Hou, H., & Tsai, C. (2012). University students' online information searching strategies in different search contexts. *Australasian Journal of Educational Technology, 28*(5), 881-895. Available from http://www.ascilite.org.au/ajet/ajet28/tsai-mj.html

Tweed, S. R. (2013). *Technology implementation: Teacher age, experience, self-efficacy, and professional development as related to classroom technology integration.* Available from http://ca.yhs4.search.yahoo.com/r/_ylt=AwrTcc4f1rlSYWEAEU4XFwx.;_ylu=X3oDMTByaDNhc2JxBHNlYwNzcgRwb3MDMQRjb2xvA2dxMQR2dGlkAw--/SIG=12npd2ve7/EXP=1387939487/**http%3a//dc.etsu.edu/cgi/viewcontent.cgi%3farticle=2266%26context=etd

Uddin, S., & Jacobson, M. (2013). Dynamics of email communications among university students throughout a semester. *Computers & Education, 64*, 95-103. Available from http://www.academia.edu/2910923/Dynamics_of_Email_Communications_among_University_Students_throughout_a_Semester

University of British Columbia. (2011). *The effectiveness of educational technology in post-secondary education, ETEC 510*, from Wiki page. Retrieved from http://sites.wiki.ubc.ca/etec510/The_Effectiveness_ofEducational_Technology_in_Post-Secondary_Education

University of Saskatchewan. (2008). *The internship: Making meaning of teaching and learning.* Saskatoon, SK: University of Saskatchewan, College of Education.

Urtel, M., & Fernandez, E. (2012). To podcast or not to podcast. In R. Morgan & K. Olivares (Eds.), *Quick hits for teaching with technology: Successful strategies by award-winning teachers* (pp. 37-38). Bloomington, IN: Indiana University Press.

Vanderveen, J. (2012). Let students design the test. In R. Morgan & K. Olivares (Eds.), *Quick hits for teaching with technology: Successful strategies by award-winning teachers* (pp. 75-76). Bloomington, IN: Indiana University Press.

Vanderveen, J., & Wells, J. (2012).Group work online. In R. Morgan & K. Olivares (Eds.), *Quick hits for teaching with technology: Successful strategies by award-winning teachers* (pp. 101-102). Bloomington, IN: Indiana University Press.

Venkatesh, V., Rabah, J., Fusaro, M., Couture, A., Varela, W., & Alexander, K. (2012, October). Perceptions of technology use and course effectiveness in the age of Web 2.0: A large-scale survey of Québec university students and instructors. *In World Conference on E-Learning in Corporate, Government, Healthcare, and Higher Education*, 2012, 1691-1699. Abstract available at http://editlib.org/noaccess/41850/

Viers, J. (2009). *Using humor as a teaching tool: A literature review and analysis*. Retrieved from http://voices.yahoo.com/using-humor-as-teaching-tool-1701219.html

Vogel, D., Kennedy, D. & Kwok, R. (2009). Does using mobile device applications lead to learning? *Journal of Interactive Learning Research, 20*(4), 469-485. Chesapeake, VA: AACE. Retrieved August 3, 2013 from http://www.editlib.org/p/29431.

Vogt, M., & Schaffner, B. (2012). Using audience response systems for classroom post-test reviews. In R. Morgan & K. Olivares (Eds.), *Quick hits for teaching with technology: Successful strategies by award-winning teachers* (p. 94-95). Bloomington, IN: Indiana University Press.

Waldron, M., & Moore, G. (1991). *Helping adults learn: Course planning for adult learners.* Toronto: Thompson.

Walls, S., Kucsera, J., Walker, J., Acee, T., McVaugh, N., & Robinson, D. (2010). Podcasting in education: Are students as ready and eager as we think they are? *Computers & Education, 54*, 371–378. Retrieved from http://www.sciencedirect.com/science/article/pii/S0360131509002140

Walsh, K. (2013, January 6). Flipped classroom successes in higher education. *EmergingEdTech.* Retrieved from http://www.emergingedtech.com/2013/01/flipped-classroom-successes-in-higher-education/

Wang, V. (2011). Effective teaching with technology in adult education. In E. Ng., N. Karacapilidis, & M. Raisinghani (Eds.), *Dynamic advancements in teaching and learning based technologies: New concepts* (pp. 264-279). Hershey, PA: Information Science Reference.

Wang Wei-Tsong, Wang, C. (2009). An empirical study of instructor adoption of web-based learning systems. *Computers & Education, 53,* 761–774. Retrieved from http://www.sciencedirect.com/science/article/pii/S0360131509001080

Warschauer, M. (2011). *Learning in the cloud: How (and why) to transform schools with digital media.* New York: Teachers College Press.

Wasserstein, A., Quistberg, D., & Shea, J. (2007). Mentoring at the University of Pennsylvania: Results of a faculty survey. *Journal of General Internal Medicine, 22*(2), 210-214. Available from http://www.ncbi.nlm.nih.gov/pmc/articles/PMC1824746/

Waters, J. (2012). The impact of instructor intervention style on student activity in asynchronous online learning discussion boards. In T. Bastiaens & G. Marks (Eds.), *Proceedings of World Conference on E-Learning in Corporate, Government, Healthcare, and Higher Education, 2012,* (pp. 831-840). Chesapeake, VA: AACE. Abstract available at http://www.editlib.org/noaccess/41698

Waycott, J., Bennett, S., Kennedy, G., Dalgarno, B., & Gray, K. (2010). Digital divides? Student and staff perceptions of information and communication technologies. *Computers & Education, 54,* 1202–1211. Retrieved from http://dx.doi.org/10.1016/j.compedu.2009.11.006

Weas, L. (2010, March 03). An exploratory study regarding the needs of adult learners for today's technological workforce & social media. *Adult Learning & Technology.* Retrieved from http://www.slideshare.net/larryweas/adult-learning-amp-technology

Weaver, R., II, & Cotrell, H. (1987). *Lecturing: Essential communication strategies.* In M. Weimer (Ed.), *Teaching large classes well* (pp. 57-70). San Francisco: Jossey-Bass.

Weber, E. (1997). Resolving small group conflicts. *The Teaching Professor, 11*(2), 4.

Weimer, M. (1990). What can discussion accomplish? In M. Weimer & R. Neff (Eds.), *Teaching college: Collected readings for the new instructor* (p. 97). Madison, WI: Magna.

Weimer, M. (1996a). Active learning: Quantity, extent, depth count. *The Teaching Professor, 10*(10), 1.

Weimer, M. (1996b). Cooperative learning and communication: Evidence of results. *The Teaching Professor, 10*(10), 5.

Weimer, M. (1996c). The ethics of teaching. *The Teaching Professor, 10*(10), 2.

Weimer, M. (1996d). Student motivation not a desperate situation. *The Teaching Professor, 10*(10), 7.

Weimer, M. (1997a). Cooperative learning & problem solving. *The Teaching Professor, 11*(1), 2.

Weimer, M. (1997b). Problem-based learning models. *The Teaching Professor, 11*(1), 4.

Weimer, M. (1997c). What makes a good teacher? *The Teaching Professor, 11*(1), 1-2.

Weller, W. (2012). Mitigating the workload and increasing student satisfaction with online discussion threads. In R. Morgan & K. Olivares (Eds.), *Quick hits for teaching with technology: Successful strategies by award-winning teachers* (pp. 89-90). Bloomington, IN: Indiana University Press.

Westerberg, C. (2013, February 15). The list: 12 top technologies in education. *The Daily Riff.* Retrieved from http://www.thedailyriff.com/articles/the-list-top-technologies-that-will-change-learning-teaching-higher-education-1021.ph

Whelan, A., Walker, R., & Moore, C. (Eds.). (2013). *Zombies in the academy: Living death in higher education.* Chicago, IL: Intellect, Ltd.

White, K., & Weight, B. (1999). *The online teaching guide: A handbook of attitudes, strategies, and techniques for the virtual classroom.* Don Mills, ON: Pearson Allyn & Bacon.

Wieling, M., & Hofman, W. (2010). The impact of online video lecture recordings and automated feedback on student performance. *Computers & Education, 54,* 992–998. Retrieved from http://www.sciencedirect.com/science/article/pii/S0360131509002784

Wiggins, G. (1993). Assessment: authenticity, context, and validity. *Phi Delta Kappan, 75,* 200-214.

Wiles, J., & Bondi, J. (2011). *Cuurriculum development: A guide to practice* (8th ed.). New York: Pearson.

Willis, J. (2006). *Research-based strategies to ignite student learning: Insights from a neurologist and classroom teacher.* Alexandria, VA: ASCD (Association for Supervision and Curriculum Development).

Williams, M., Foulger, T., & Wetzel, K. (2009). Preparing preservice teachers for 21st century classrooms: Transforming attitudes and behaviors about innovative technology. *Journal of Technology and Teacher Education, 17*(3), 393-418. Chesapeake, VA: SITE. Retrieved August 2, 2013 from http://www.editlib.org/p/28216

Wilson, D., & Conyers, M. (2013). *Five big ideas for effective teaching: Connecting mind, brain, and education research to classroom practice.* New York: Teachers College Press.

Windschitl, M. (2002). The challenges of sustaining a constructivist classroom culture. In K. Cauley, F. Linder, & J. McMillan (Eds.), *Annual editions: Educational psychology 02/03* (17th ed., pp. 97-102). Guilford, CT: McGraw-Hill Dushkin.

Wise, A. (Ed.). (1996). Quality teaching for the 21st century [entire issue]. *Phi Delta Kappan, 78*(3).

Wlodkowski, R. (2011). *Enhancing adult motivation to learn: A comprehensive guide for teaching all adults* (3rd ed.). San Francisco: Jossey-Bass.

Wohlfarth, D., & Mitchell, N. (2012).Techiquette: The etiquette of technology. In R. Morgan & K. Olivares (Eds.), *Quick hits for teaching with technology: Successful strategies by award-winning teachers* (p. 90). Bloomington, IN: Indiana University Press. [that they feel relieved to understand the often unwritten and unsaid rules that guide our use of technology. And personally, we found it is easier to nudge a student to behave with technological manners when the rules of the game have been previously agreed upon.]

Wohlfarth, D., Morgan, D., & Mitchell, N. (2012).That's why they call it YOUTube. In R. Morgan & K. Olivares (Eds.), *Quick hits for teaching with technology: Successful strategies by award-winning teachers* (pp. 13-14). Bloomington, IN: Indiana University Press.

Won Park, J. (2012). The simple visual mapping tool for thinking aloud. In R. Morgan & K. Olivares (Eds.), *Quick hits for teaching with technology: Successful strategies by award-winning teachers* (pp. 20-21). Bloominton, IN: Indiana University Press.

Worthen, B. (1993). Critical issues that will determine the future of authentic assessment. *Phi Delta Kappan, 74*, 444-454.

Wozniak, H., & Silveira, S. (2004). Online discussions: Promoting effective student to student interaction. In *Beyond the comfort zone: Proceedings of the 21st ASCILITE Conference 2004* (pp. 956–960). Available from http://www.ascilite.org.au/conferences/perth04/procs/wozniak.html

Wray, F. (2012). Using Prezi to produce creative critical thinking assessments. In R. Morgan & K. Olivares (Eds.), *Quick hits for teaching with technology: Successful strategies by award-winning teachers* (p. 69-70). Bloomington, IN: Indiana University Press.

Yamane, D. (1997). Group projects: Problems and possible solutions. *The Teaching Professor, 11*(2), 5.

Yang, D., & Richardson, J. (2010). Online interaction styles: Adapting to active interaction styles. In H. Yang & S. Yuen (Eds.), *Handbook of research on practices and outcomes in e-learning: Issues and trends* (pp. 138-149). Hershey, PA: Information Science Reference.

Yang, H. H., & Yuen, S. C. (Eds.). (2010). *Handbook of research on practices and outcomes in e-learning: Issues and trends.* Hershey, PA: Information Science Reference.

Yelon, S. (2006). *Lessons learned from excellent teachers: Ten powerful instructional principles.* Michigan State University, College of Human Medicine. Retrieved from http://www.digitalpresentations.org/Handouts/Yelon_handout.pdf

Yorke, J. (Ed.) (2011). *Meeting the challenges.* Proceedings of the ATN (Australian Technology Network) Assessment Conference, 20-21 October, Perth, Western Australia: Curtin University. Retrieved from

https://eprints.usq.edu.au/21515/1/Lawson_Taylor_Fallshaw_etal_ATNA_2011_PV.pdf

Young, F. (2012, November 28). 35 digital tools that work with bloom's taxonomy. *Edudemic.* Retrieved from http://www.edudemic.com/2012/11/35-digital-tools-that-work-with-blooms-taxonomy/

Yu, W., Sun, Y., & Chang Y. (2010). When technology speaks language: An evaluation of course management systems used in a language learning context. *ReCALL, 22*(03), 332- 350. Retrieved from http://journals.cambridge.org/action/displayFulltext?type=6&fid=7884178&jid=REC&volumeId=22&is

sueId=03&aid=7884177&bodyId=&membershipNumber=&societyETOC Session=&fulltextType=RA&fileId=S0958344010000194

Zhan, Z., Xu, F., & Ye, H. (2011). Effects of an online learning community on active and reflective learners' learning performance and attitudes in a face-to-face undergraduate course. *Computers and Education, 56*(4), 961-968. doi: 10.1016/j.compedu.2010.11.012. Retrieved from http://www.sciencedirect.com/science/article/pii/S0360131510003337

Zink, A. (2012). Google-Doc surveys for teaching Hispanic culture. In R. Morgan & K. Olivares (Eds.), *Quick hits for teaching with technology: Successful strategies by award-winning teachers* (p. 65). Bloomington, IN: Indiana University Press.

Ziv, A. (1998). Teaching and learning with humor: Experiment and replication. *The Journal of Experimental Education, 57*(1), pp. 5-15. Retrieved from http://www.jstor.org/stable/20151750

Zygouris-Coe, V., Swan, B., & Ireland, J. (2009). Online learning and quality assurance. *International Journal on E-Learning, 8*(1), 127-146. Chesapeake, VA: AACE. Retrieved August 2, 2013 from http://www.editlib.org/p/25228

About the Authors

Dr. Jay Wilson is an associate professor in the Curriculum Studies Department as the University of Saskatchewan. He has extensive practical experience in the areas of technology and instruction and has been honoured with a number of teaching awards for his efforts. He has worked to raise the profile of teaching in higher education. His program of research centres on authentic learning, design studio learning, and technology skill development in educators.

Edwin Ralph is a professor and internship facilitator with the College of Education at the University of Saskatchewan. He is an award-winning teacher and his teaching and research interests lie in the areas of instructional improvement, learning motivation, and mentorship across the professions.

www.ingramcontent.com/pod-product-compliance
Lightning Source LLC
Chambersburg PA
CBHW050804160426
43192CB00010B/1641